Developing Student Capability Through Modular Courses

The Teaching and Learning in Higher Education Series
Series Editor: John Stephenson

Developing Student Capability Through Modular Courses

EDITED BY
**Alan Jenkins and
Lawrie Walker**

Routledge
Taylor & Francis Group

LONDON AND NEW YORK

First published in 1994 by Kogen Page Limited

Published 2019 by Routledge
2 Park Square, Milton Park, Abingdon, Oxon OX14 4RN
52 Vanderbilt Avenue, New York, NY 10017

Routledge is an imprint of the Taylor & Francis Group, an informa business

British Library Cataloguing in Publication Data

A CIP record for this book is available from the British Library.
ISBN 0 7494 1369 7

Typeset by Saxon Graphics Ltd, Derby

ISBN 13: 978-0-7494-1369-9 ((pbk)

Contents

6

SECTION D: LARGE-SCALE SOLUTIONS

SECTION E: TOWARDS THE FUTURE

Acknowledgements

This book grew out of a conference jointly organized by Oxford Brookes University and Higher Education for Capability. Many people gave their time to this conference – in particular Alison Little and John Stephenson of Education for Capability. Much of the typing was done by Hilary Churchley.

Preface

John Stephenson

The current interest in curriculum change sweeping through higher education – and further education – is a response to demands for the development of personal qualities and skills related to the world of work, ever-tightening resource constraints coupled with external assessments of the quality of provision, and the accumulation of awareness of good practice in teaching and learning. Indeed, much of our awareness of how further and higher education might be improved has been with us for some time. What is new is the commitment of institutions to introduce new practices across a wide range of their courses.

A major feature of these developments is an emphasis on the development of student autonomy in learning. Rapidly changing circumstances at work and in society are putting a premium on adaptability, working together and learning from experience. In the UK, national movements such as Higher Education for Capability (an initiative which originated in the Royal Society for the encouragement of Arts, Manufacturers and Commerce (RSA) and is now based in Leeds Metropolitan University and the University of Leeds) and the Department of Employment's Enterprise in Higher Education initiative have stimulated much innovation. In North America and Australasia, similar pressure for enhancing the quality and relevance of provision is provoking a similar response.

Interest in restructuring university courses into modules or standardized interchangeable units has grown rapidly in the UK since the 1970s. The motivation for these changes includes a desire to provide more flexible responses to the needs and aspirations of the greater variety of students now entering higher education, to make separate components of courses more readily available to outside groups and to make more efficient use of expensive units of resources. Institutions have had to address important educational issues such as the identification of intermediate levels of achievement, learning outcomes, forms of assessment and student guidance systems. Though many enthusiasts for capability approaches to learning have taken the opportunity presented by the switch to modular structures to give students responsibility for their own learning, this has not been the norm. The learning experiences of many students have remained much the same as they were before modularization took place – except they are likely to be assessed more frequently.

If we want to use higher education to enhance student capability, the challenge is to group the opportunity presented by the modularization of courses to change the nature of the relationship between tutors and students in favour of more participative modes of learning and to enable students to engage more directly with key learning processes such as planning and reviewing their own progress, assessing their own and their peers' performance, relating to the needs of the wider community and developing personal skills and qualities.

The examples of some current developments in modular courses featured in this book were originally presented at a national conference, Using Modularity to Develop Student Capability, organized by Higher Education for Capability (HEC) in association with Oxford Brookes University. We believe that others can learn from these experiences, particularly if new ideas and approaches are seen to be in operation and not just in somebody's imagination. We begin with an overview of the issues in the Introduction. We then present a range of examples grouped under four themes: developing modular frameworks; core modules and core skills; developing skills through student choice and independent study; and large-scale solutions. Finally, in Section E we explore some of the implications for universities and consider ways in which modular programmes might develop.

The Teaching and Learning in Higher Education series will be of interest to all with responsibility for the design and delivery of the curriculum. We do not present blueprints or models of good practice. We offer glimpses of what others are doing and what they have learned from doing it, leaving readers to judge their relevance and adapt their implementation to their own circumstances. If readers know of other examples which would add to understanding of the issues raised in this book, please send them to Alison Little, HEC, 20 Queen Square, Leeds LS2 8AF, UK. HEC provides an information service on current practice in further and higher education aimed at promoting the development of student capability.

Contributors

Linda Bonnet is a Senior Teaching Fellow in the Department of Biochemistry and Molecular Biology at the University of Leeds, with 17 years' undergraduate teaching experience with science and medical students. She is a member of the department's Innovative Teaching Group and has fulfilled roles as: Final Year Combined Studies Course Tutor; Admissions Tutor (latterly coordinator of admissions to all departmental undergraduate programmes and Chair of the Departmental Recruitment Group); and a three-year half-time secondment to the university's Office of Part-time Education, during which she initiated the development of part-time degrees in science.

Sarah Brierley is currently President of Oxford Brookes Students' Union. Previously she served as a sabbatical and non-sabbatical executive officer, a student representative and as chair of a hall of residence committee.

Dave Brookes graduated from Oxford Polytechnic in 1992 and then worked for a year as the Student Enterprise Coordinator. He now works for Lloyds Bank.

Peter Burke worked as a school teacher and then became chief executive of the Southern Examination Group, responsible for the introduction of the GCSE examination system. He is now an independent consultant.

Adrian Carey is currently deputy head of the Surrey TVEI extension project. His own experiences of teaching across a wide range of abilities and ages have convinced him of the benefits of shorter units of learning and assessment objectives which are clear to both the learner and the teacher. Together with Peter Burke he was a founder member of the Modular Information Network (MIN) in the mid-1980s and played a key role in the development of modular schemes in Surrey. He continues to promote the cause of modularity and currently chairs the executive group of the MIN. He contributed to the Further Education Unit's 'A Basis for Credit?' discussion document and works to promote opportunities for learning which equip individuals with the characteristics of lifetime learners.

Judy Chance is a Senior Lecturer in the Geography Unit at Oxford Brookes University. Her main teaching responsibilities lie in research and investigative methodologies, the social geography of race and ethnicity, the impact of globalization on developing countries and the geography of Japan. In common with the other members of the unit, she is committed to the development of student-centred learning.

Graham Gaskell graduated from Oxford Polytechnic in 1991. He was an executive officer at Oxford Brookes Students' Union from 1991–3, first as Deputy President Campaigns/Welfare, and then as President. During his time as a student he served as a non-sabbatical executive officer, was a joint chair of RAG, sat as a student representative on the Academic Board, and held several part-time jobs. He is currently Student Enterprise Coordinator.

Chris Gore is Associate Head (Head of Undergraduate Programmes), Coventry Business School, Coventry University. She has published extensively on topics related to strategic management and the enterprise culture. Her wide teaching experience at both undergraduate and postgraduate level has provided the basis for the development of several distance-learning texts and other publications on general education issues.

Richard Horobin, who has a wide range of teaching interests, is currently Reader in the Department of Biomedical Science at Sheffield University. As well as teaching medical, dental and science students within the university, he has over many years designed and taught courses in laboratory technology for various external organizations.

John Hughes, who has a background in teaching in secondary schools and further education, was previously the BP Fellow for Student Tutoring at Imperial College (University of London). He is now seconded to BP to manage the International Mentoring and Tutoring Project as part of BP's Community and Educational Relations team. The project supports the development of student tutoring programmes worldwide as well as mentoring programmes involving BP staff working with young people. John is a Fellow of the Royal Society for the Arts, an Associate Member of the Institute of Electrical Engineers and is active in the Association for Science Education.

Alan Jenkins taught geography in the modular course at Oxford Brookes. He now works in its Educational Methods Unit on staff development teaching and in Enterprise with a particular responsibility for helping devise a way of profiling all undergraduates. His publications include (with David Pepper) *Enhancing Employability and Educational Opportunity* (1987, Birmingham SCED); and (with Graham Gibbs) *Teaching Large Classes in Higher Education* (1992, Kogan Page).

Mike Laycock is Enterprise Director at the University of East London. He was formerly Course Tutor for the undergraduate and then postgraduate programmes in the School for Independent Study at the University. His recent publications include (with Professor John Stephenson) *Using Learning Contracts in Higher Education* (1993, Kogan Page); and 'Enterprise in higher education and learner-managed learning' in Graves, N (ed.) *Learner-managed learning: policy, theory and Practice* (1993, HEC, Leeds).

Marilyn Leask is a Senior Lecturer in Education at Bedford College of Higher Education. Her interests are in enhancing the quality of educational provision through the development of reflective management practices. Her recent book (with Del Goddard), *The Search for Quality: Planning improvement and managing Change* (1992, Paul Chapman Publishing), provides an analysis of change in the UK educational context. Currently she is working on cross-national comparisons of the management of change in education.

David Longworth is the Subject Leader for Geography in the Department of Environmental Management at the University of Central Lancashire. He has a wide range of teaching experience in geography, including aspects of pedagogy and the relationships between geography and education. His main research interests are in glacial and montane geomorphology and he is academic adviser to the university's Scientific Expedition Society, having participated in ventures ranging from the Grand Tetons of North America to the Tien Shan of Central Asia. He is committed to the development of active practical learning experiences for undergraduates in field, laboratory and computer contexts.

Kate Murray is Acting Dean of the Derbyshire Business School, University of Derby. She came into higher education with a background in economic analysis and the provision of direct investment venture capital. She has written extensively in the areas of business education, economic analysis and strategic decision-making.

Rob Pope is currently a Principal Lecturer in English Studies at Oxford Brookes University. He has previously taught in universities in Wales and Russia, and is the author of *How to Study Chaucer* (1988, Macmillan) and *Textual Intervention: Critical and creative strategies for literary studies* (1994, Routledge).

Clive Robertson is currently Head of Quality Assurance in the Faculty of Business, Languages and Hotel Management at Oxford Brookes University. He chairs the university's Credit Accumulation and Transfer committee. His research and consultancy interests include experiential and action learning, and the accreditation of work-based learning including the use of work-based contracts.

Brian Roper is an economist by training and has extensive experience of higher education management. Brian was previously Deputy Vice-

Chancellor for Academic Affairs at Oxford Brookes University and is now Vice-Chancellor of the University of North London.

David Scurry is currently Dean of the Modular Course at Oxford Brookes University and Chair of the Group of Deans and Directors of Modular Courses. He has been involved in the validation of many modular degree schemes and has also been chief external examiner for a number of modular schemes. He has extensive knowledge of the different types and styles of modular courses that are offered in the UK and has represented the UK in discussions organized by the EU about the transfer of academic credit within Europe.

David Turner is Assistant Dean of the Modular Course at Oxford Brookes University and as such has particular responsibility for examination committees and admissions with credit. His background is in chemistry and he has been on the committee of the Assessment Group of the Royal Society of Chemistry for a number of years.

Mike Vaughan was, at the time of the project, Head of Credit Systems at the University of Wolverhampton. He has specific responsibility for the accessibility and vocational orientation of university provision, including off-site learning, and has been active nationally in a number of developments implementing Credit Accumulation and Transfer Systems.

Lawrie Walker is currently Director of the Enterprise Programme at Oxford Brookes University. Prior to this he was Director of the Technical and Vocational Initiative in Oxfordshire and a member of the LEA Senior Advisory Team. Over the last 13 years he has managed a series of externally-funded curriculum projects with schools, colleges and higher education institutions.

Hugh Wilkins joined the School of Hotel and Catering Management at Oxford Brookes University in 1989 from Staffordshire Polytechnic Management Centre. Prior to working in education he had worked in industry and as a consultant, as well as owning and operating a public house and restaurant. He originally graduated as an economist from the London School of Economics.

Mike Williams holds a Personal Chair in Anatomical Science. He has been teaching medical and science students for about 30 years, having played a large part in the founding and development of a widely-known degree course, the Special Honours BSc in Anatomy and Cell Biology.

Harvey Woolf is currently Head of Modular Development in the University of Wolverhampton's Unit for the Coordination of Academic Initiatives. An historian by background, he has been involved in the management of modular schemes for nearly 20 years; is an external examiner for three modular/combined studies programmes and has served on numerous validation panels for such schemes. He was a member of the university's Enterprise in the Humanities curriculum development team, which won one of the first Partnership Awards, and is Vice-Chair of the university's Quality Assurance Committee.

Glossary

APL	Accreditation of Prior Learning
APEL	Assessment of Prior Experiential Learning
BTEC	Business and Technology Education Council
CATS	Credit Accumulation and Transfer Scheme
CBL	Computer-based Learning
CGLI	City and Guilds London Institute
CNAA	Council for National Academic Awards
CVCP	Vice-Chancellers and Principals Committee
DipHE	Diploma in Higher Education
EHE	Enterprise in Higher Education
ET	Employment Training
ERASMUS	European Community Action Scheme for the Mobility of University Students
FEU	Further Education Unit
GCE	General Certificate of Education
GCSE	General Certificate of Secondary Education
GNVQ	General National Vocational Qualification
HE	Higher Education
HEC	Higher Education for Capability
HEFC(E)	Higher Education Funding Council (England)
HEI	Higher Education Institute
HMI	Her Majesty's Inspectorate
HNC	Higher National Certificate
HND	Higher National Diploma
MBA	Master of Business Administration
MIN	Modular Information Network
NIACE	National Institute of Adult Continuing Education
NTET	National Training and Education Targets
NCVQ	National Council for Vocational Qualifications
NVQ	National Vocational Qualification
RSA	Royal Society of Arts
SEAC	School Examinations and Assessment Council
SEC	Secondary Examinations Council
TEVI	Technical and Vocational Education Initiative
TEXT	Trans European Exchange and Transfer Consortium

UDACE   Unit for the Development of Adult Continuing Education
UFC   Universities Funding Council

Chapter One

Introduction

Alan Jenkins and Lawrie Walker

The modular structure makes it difficult, but not impossible to ensure the systematic development of interpersonal and communication skills.

(DES, 1991, p .8)

This was the judgement of a visiting panel of Her Majesty's Inspectors on the modular course at Oxford Polytechnic (now Oxford Brookes), one of the pioneering modular courses in the UK. The fear that modular courses result in intellectual fragmentation and make difficult the coherent and progressive development of student skills is one that is shared by many academics.

The basic principles of modular courses are now well known and established: they involve the division of the curriculum into limited units or modules of learning which are then assessed at the end of that unit, with the student building up a degree or award through such learning being credited.

Oxford Polytechnic's modular course began in 1972. Then such modular schemes were rare in British higher education. Now most higher education institutions in the UK are moving towards some kind of modular provision. Much of the impetus for this 'container revolution' comes from a drive for efficiency as institutions seek to lower teaching and administration costs to deal with a declining unit of resource and achieve expansion of student numbers. There are also strong educational arguments for modular courses – these are explored by Lawrie Walker in Chapter 2 – but they are often subordinated to institutional requirements and arguments for efficiency.

Incompatible initiatives?

British higher education is replete with initiatives and policies, most of them from government and higher education funding bodies. Some of these initiatives support and reinforce each other. For example, policies to ensure a more skilled workforce reinforce policies to open up higher education to groups hitherto excluded. Other polices clash and contend. For example policies that require institutions to audit and assess their teaching effectiveness are developed at the same time as research assessment exercises. These immediately support individuals and departments that subordinate a concern for students to a desire to gain the rewards from a higher grade in the next research assessment exercise.

This book explores ways of reconciling two of these developments in British higher education. At the same time, as most HE institutions are going modular they are under increasing pressure from government, funding bodies and students themselves to ensure that their courses enable students to develop 'capability' – the skills and attitudes that empower them as lifelong learners and that give them an edge in a competitive labour market.

Modular structures can weaken, even imperil the development of student capability. Modular courses emphasize packaging knowledge into discrete units which can too often be soon forgotten. Modular courses generally emphasize student choice and flexible course patterns. Capability/skill development may best be developed through a coherent, systematic curriculum that some might see is best achieved through the traditional subject-based linear degree.

Student perspectives

When we asked students at Oxford Brookes about their experience of skill development in a modular framework, their comments picked out problems that we think would be represented in many and perhaps all modular courses (Jenkins and Rust, 1993). They saw modular courses as enshrining their choice of what (if not how) to learn. Students who were studying two subjects (fields) tended to see these as quite separate areas of knowledge. A student who had studied business and accounts saw 'no real pattern' to his learning. He was learning more but it was all 'higgledy piggledy'. Two first-year students could see no point, no relation, between the modules they took outside earth sciences to the programme of studies within that field. A geography student told us that many of her friends avoided modules which required them to work in groups. Even if these students saw these modules as helping them to practise key (employability) skills, they perceived themselves as weak in these areas and sought to avoid such courses. Often the modular structure allowed them to make that choice.

Many students commented that certain skills – in particular group work – were encountered again and again, but with little or no training and no sense of progression and limited or non-existent feedback. As they and the staff finished a module the were on to the next batch with no time or opportunity for reflection and feedback.

One might conclude from these comments, and those of staff and students in other modular courses, that in their emphasis on flexibility and choice modular courses to an extent disempower students and certainly do not necessarily lead to more skilful/capable students. Yet other comments (often by the same students) saw modular courses as enabling and even developing their capability. A recurrent theme was that modular courses developed their ability to manage time and tasks. The philosophy of choice made them feel more responsible for their learning while the term assessments made them work hard and consistently. Students from a wide range of subjects described how skills had been integrated into the way those subjects were taught and assessed. Furthermore, some students were using the choice offered by modular programmes to build up a portfolio of skills and abilities. A few were aware of university-wide discussions to better integrate and develop transferable skills throughout the modular course.

Reconciling modularity and student capability

We are critical of the traditional British degree structure. Coherence was often more in the view of staff than in the experience of students. Staff needs for disciplinary boundaries and coherence often took precedence over student needs. Seldom were transferable/employability skills clearly developed in such degree programmes.

However, we do recognize that modular courses can easily lead to intellectual incoherence and fragmentation. This book is based on the belief that modular courses can be designed so as to build in a capability perspective. The organization of the book shows how we consider this can be achieved by subject groups and by whole institutions. In Section A we consider how institutional structures can be designed to develop learner autonomy and student employability. We also briefly consider how modular developments in schools and further education will shape those students' experiences before they enter higher education.

In Section B our scale of observation is that of the subject group. From a variety of disciplinary perspectives we see how skills can be progressively developed through core modules and by disciplines defining and developing core skills.

In Section C we show how a basic principle of modular courses – that of crediting learning – can be its greatest strength in developing student capability. We consider the experience of a variety of institutions that have used modular credits to value and develop a wide range of skills. The particular initiatives differ, varying from students working in local schools to students helping other students to develop information technology skills. All these initiatives show how choice and modular credits can be used to develop capability.

In Section D our perspective is that of the whole institution or a large department or faculty. Again the initiatives are particular: rewriting all modules/courses in a common format using learning outcomes; getting students and staff to reflect and communicate what is the reality of the student experience; using learning contracts and/or profiling as a way to help the students coherently develop their skills through large modular courses. Though these particular initiatives vary they share the common aim of ensuring that large modular structures and course requirements enable student capability.

Finally, in Section E, we look to the future of modular schemes in Britain and the emerging European and international credit frameworks.

Beyond British experience

All of the case studies reported here are British and grow out of the immediate pressures of British higher education. For those of us in the UK there is a danger of seeing these changes from a very insular perspective. We should remind ourselves that many national higher education structures are modular. The ideas for the Oxford Polytechnic's 'pioneering' modular course grew out of the knowledge of West African and North American experience of its first Dean, David Mobbs. In North America the idea of crediting student effort by hours studied (Carnegie units) developed in the late 19th century. Through a complex but interlocking structure, the North American higher education system offers students choice to develop and credit their learning by moving in and out of institutions throughout their lives. North America shows others the 'value' and the 'efficiency' of these modular arrangements. They also remind us that modular courses can lapse into bureaucracy and intellectual incoherence. An American study of US higher education reported that:

> The curriculum has given way to a marketplace philosophy: it is the supermarket where students are shoppers and professors are merchants of learning. Fads and fashion, the demands of popularity and success, enter where experience should prevail .... The marketplace philosophy refuses to establish certain common expectations and norms .... It is as if no one cared as long as the store stayed open.
>
> (*Association of American Colleges*, 1985, pp. 2–3)

In 1993 a high-level report echoed a similar critique. The report, 'An American imperative: higher expectations for higher education', argued that 'Much too frequently, American higher education offered a smorgasbord of fanciful courses in a fragmented curriculum'. Amongst its recommendations are for institutions and subject groups to clearly define the learning outcomes and 'knowledge skills and abilities' they expect of graduates (*Chronicle of Higher Education*, 1993). Prompted by these critiques, contemporary North American higher education offers a whole series of initiatives to ensure coherence and progressive skills development within modular credit framework. Many institutions have moved to ideas of a core curriculum, often in general education programmes (Graff, 1991). At both federal and state levels there are moves to define core skills that all students should develop. Innovative programmes are being developed at many institutions to provide their own framework to extend student abilities and these are often reported in journals such as *Change, Chronicle of Higher Education* and *The College Professor*.

British modular courses can learn much from this rich and varied experience. In turn we hope readers outside the UK can benefit from the issues and case studies reported here. We are early learners in these territories of modularity and skills, but we are learning fast.

References

Association of American Colleges (1985) *Integrity in the College Curriculum*, Washington DC: Association of American Colleges.

Chronicle of Higher Education (1993), 'An American imperative: higher expectations for higher education', December 8, A26.

Department of Education and Science (1991) *The Modular Course at Oxford Polytechnic: A report by HMI*, Stanmore, Middlesex: DES.

Graff, J G (1991) *New Life for the College Curriculum*, San Francisco, CA: Jossey Bass.

Jenkins, A and Rust, C (1993) 'Modular Courses and Students' Transferable Skills: Perspectives from Oxford Brookes University', Educational Methods Unit, Oxford Brookes University. (This video can be purchased from the Education Methods Unit, Oxford Brookes University, Oxford OX3 OBP.)

SECTION A:
DEVELOPING MODULAR FRAMEWORKS

Chapter 2

The New Higher Education Systems, Modularity and Student Capability

Lawrie Walker

The modular argument

For two decades modularity in the British education system has advanced and retreated like waves on a beach. In higher education the waves are washing at the base of very old cliffs. Modularity is fashionable. The reasons are well-rehearsed – new clients with new needs and mixed modes of study, customer choice, credit frameworks, blurring boundaries between academic disciplines, new integrations between 'academic' and 'vocational' programmes, the pressure of Assessment of Prior Experiential Learning (APEL) and National Vocational Qualifications (NVQs) – and a claimed cost-effectiveness.

The curricular case for well-designed modular programmes is also well-rehearsed – student choice, learner autonomy, flexibility for individual student circumstances, adaptability to new modes of learning and assessment, speed of response to external pressures and agencies, openness to new kinds of knowledge and new connections. As with all things, however, its potential strengths are its possible weaknesses. Poorly designed modular programmes are vulnerable to intellectual incoherence, to problems with continuity and progression of learning, to loss of student identity and to excessive bureaucracy. It may be that such charges can equally be levelled at some non-modular courses (coherence is not guaranteed by length of course and lack of student choice) but it seems true that modular programmes are prone to fragmentation unless carefully designed and monitored.

This book is about the promotion of 'capability' in students who are studying on modular course. 'Capability', like 'enterprise' and 'lifelong learning' is something of a catchall: if it is going to be a criterion it will need to be defined. When I think of the word 'capability' I think of 'Capability' Brown, who designed landscapes which combined technical skill, beauty and utility with natural elegance. At each turn a new combination of shape, colour, texture, a subtle exposure, a hidden stream, an open vista, a closure round a statute or a building, a lake curving behind a wooded hill, hints and revelations: and all planned to develop over time with trees and flowers whose full shapes and interleavings were seen only by later generations. That combination of imagination and skill which could comprehend material, space and time in a practical vision earned him his name. If I may extrapolate from a long-dead man to our extremely lively undergraduates, I define capability as the ability to turn ideas into action through knowledge, imagination and skill. To do that people need information and the knowledge to find and use information; they have to be able to plan and carry through their intentions; they require technical and professional skills and the skills to persuade people to take their ideas seriously, to work with others towards a common end; and they need the courage and independence to carry their work forward and test it against the judgement of others. Knowledge alone is insufficient.

If modular programmes are to be measured against their ability to develop students who are capable in the sense described above then we must be very clear about the strengths and weaknesses inherent in modularity.

Types of modular provision

Let us begin with the bigger picture. The way in which a university structures its modular provision will affect the choices open to students and the extent to which staff can interplay different kinds of knowledge and experiences.

Universities would appear to be designing modular provision within three basic boundaries: the modular course, where an individual course is modularized without any formal relationship to other courses; the modular field or faculty, where groups of related courses are modularized within a common framework and allow for cross-access; and the modular degree, where all courses operate within a common set of modular regulations. These are rather like Chinese boxes or Russian dolls, where one can fit over the other, as long as the biggest is designed first – otherwise there is a lot of makeshift carpentry later on. Indeed, one of the more fascinating aspects of a university embarked on wholesale modularization is the process of intellectual jobbing or 'territorial smudge', whereby old, firm boundaries are held and ceded and young, uneasy alliances are formed, where creative energy is released in some staff and defences are maintained by others. In that underdetermined period between subject autonomy and collective responsibility the reality of student choice is formed.

Modular programmes develop over time under complex social pressures and are prone to continual redefinition, reinforced by the speed at which modules are introduced, deleted, modified and combined. Universities newly embarking on modularization, often at great speed with little staff development and few additional resources, go through difficult shifts of practice to accommodate new styles of learning – see, for instance, Leask, Chapter 4 in this volume. Yet as modular provision within a university becomes more sophisticated a paradox begins to appear: expertise brings confidence to try out new ideas, yet the success of the system and the weight of administrative mechanisms can act as a brake on radicalism.

The examples of modular practice described in this book have all been shaped by the political realities of academic life; some are the result of opportunism, others of planned developments within an agreed framework; each has been liberated or hindered by the modular structure and principles operating within the university.

One might categorize modular systems by their patterns of access, delivery and credit. A Mark I system is characterized by students engaged in taught modules on largely prescribed pathways within a common set of assessment regulations. Mark II introduces the accreditation of prior learning and credit accumulation and transfer, encourages part-time learning opportunities, experiments with a wider range of learning methods (self-supported study, learning contracts, peer-tutoring and so on) and provides inter- and extra-disciplinary modules. Mark III, which no British university has yet perfected, offers a sophisticated credit arrangement for prior learning and experience (including NVQ), designs joint programmes with other educational institutions and with industry and commerce, experiments with a wide range of assessment and recording methods (work-based profiles, portfolios – and so on) and assesses on demand in relation to contracted learning outcomes.

It is tempting to see a natural progression in modular provision from a carefully controlled, largely discipline-based curriculum to a flexible, negotiable system of learning contracts, and to argue that a university which has not evolved its 'modular knowledge' over time should not leap towards Mark III. But universities do not progress smoothly and all together like a well-organized army on manoeuvres. Much of the tension and triumph inferred from examples in this book can be attributed to Mark II and III developments struggling within Mark I contexts.

Capability, modularity, employability

One should not confuse capability with employability. One is larger than the other. Capable graduates are, however, more likely to do well in employment; and at a time of relatively high graduate unemployment, with universities competing for students who are increasingly bearing the financial costs of their learning, the issue of graduate employment becomes central to a university's mission and survival. To what extent can modularity improve a university's capacity to help its graduates prepare to find work and succeed in it? Is a modular system intrinsically more capable of encouraging the knowledge, skills, attitudes and experiences which empower graduates?

There is growing consensus in the United Kingdom about the characteristics of an employable graduate (Eggins, 1992). The terms used to describe particular facets of a 'desirable graduate' (from a potential employer's point of view) often differ: words such as 'skills', 'competences', 'abilities', 'capabilities' and 'attitudes' are undoubtedly coins of a common set but their values are often ambiguous. Nevertheless, most graduate recruiters would probably welcome a graduate who, as well as possessing some mastery of knowledge necessary for a given job:

- demonstrates intellectual ability (recognizes a need to know and knows how to find, interpret and use knowledge);
- learns actively and independently (can identify his or her own learning styles and needs, and the means of meeting them);
- has good self-management (can set targets, manage priorities, deal with stress, work to deadlines, etc);
- is proficient in a range of transferable, general skills (information technology, problem-solving, teamwork, financial skills, numeracy, etc);
- has experience of working, understands something of the nature of working relationships, and has strategies for dealing with personal career decisions;
- understands and can communicate personal abilities and achievements demonstrated while at university.

A university improves the graduate's chance of finding and succeeding in employment when it offers more than the development of disciplinary knowledge – though a great deal can in fact be delivered through the teaching and learning methods of a discipline. Current wisdom suggests that a university attempting to maximize the chances of its graduates doing well in their subsequent careers would provide a range of services to students, including the development of the following: learner autonomy; skills and knowledge; an understanding of the nature of work; and the use of profiling and records of achievement.

The development of learner autonomy

If capability means anything it means being able to control your own learning, set your own goals and be responsible for your own achievements – knowing your strengths and weaknesses as a learner. All universities can encourage (but not guarantee) this by the way courses are designed and delivered:

- clear learning outcomes for all courses, so that students are aware of what they are entering into and what is expected of them, can check their progress and can evaluate the effectiveness of teaching and learning;

- opportunities to enter into learning contracts which take account of personal learning choices;
- active learning styles which place a premium on student involvement in the design, delivery and assessment of learning;
- formal attention to the way students are required to be conscious of their own learning styles and strategies.

Although there would appear to be, at first sight, no appreciable difference between modular and non-modular programmes in their ability to guarantee these, there are subtle differences which may add up to a significant distinction.

All courses can be expressed in learning outcomes (Vaughan and Woolf, Chapter 13, and Wilkins, Chapter 14 in this volume). Perhaps the real difference lies in the way that modular study *necessitates* a continual negotiation of curricular coherence. Indeed, it could be claimed that students are unable to control their own learning progression within a modular programme which does not have clearly stated learning outcomes. Choice may be a condition for autonomy but it does not guarantee it.

Learning contacts, too, can be developed within any course, modular or otherwise, but the flexibility of modular provision can perhaps accommodate a wider set if options for free-standing learning contracts such as independent study modules, skills-based modules, or credited extracurricular learning (Laycock, Chapter 15, and Murray and Gore, Chapter 9 in this volume). The facility of modular provision for learning contracts is partly structural (modular pathways can more easily incorporate 'one-off' learning experiences) but mainly cultural. The culture of an established modular undergraduate programme is essentially liberating. Disciplines are respected, they form the main network of the degree (the motorways, if you like) but they are not autonomous. Students move in and out of modules which are not integral to their major disciplines but are important for their own learning requirements. Validation panels are made up of academics from other disciplines, who ask hard questions about the accessibility of modules to all students. Interdisciplinary modules are developed in response to new, problematic areas of intellectual and social discourse. Extra-disciplinary core modules (such as career insight) are offered to any student. Within such a culture, creativity is not only encouraged, it is forced into action by the dynamics of the system. The university's management task is to organize quality assurance mechanisms in such a way that the creativity springs from grounds of order: to ensure that the road system is properly planned to support the traffic of students on their way to differing destinations.

Active learning is certainly not exclusive to modular courses but there is a sense in which the mathematics of modular choice lead students to encounter a wider range of teachers and therefore of learning methods. The downside of this is, again, the possibility that learning experiences will be randomly encountered ('Not *another* group project!'). Repetition does not equal development. Students on modular courses are in fact well aware of the strengths and weaknesses of modular progression, as students from Oxford Brookes testify in the Introduction.

Yet there is a deeper issue than this, which any modular provision must come to terms with. Effective formal learning (that which is designed, purposely and directed by teachers and undertaken by identified students) requires structure, shape, continuity, coherence, economy of effort and maximization of result. Active learning will not of itself guarantee mastery. The designers of modular courses are always aware of opportunity costs, the balance between the richness and excitement of learner-driven choice and the progressive, reflective, long-term nature of intellectual development. In a modular course of study the student has greater responsibility to make the intellectual connections which make a whole of disparate parts. This can only be done by 'professionalizing' the student. By this I mean we ask the student to see learning itself as the undergraduate career, whatever the disciplines studied. Helping a student to balance active learning with reflective judgement is perhaps the most underestimated challenge to universities engaged in modular teaching. The most potentially powerful technique for achieving this is profiling. More of that below.

Learner autonomy is not learner isolation. One of the most welcome developments in recent years is the recognition being given to the way students help each other to learn (Hughes, Chapter 10, and Longworth, Chapter 11 in this volume). Module credits given to students who act as mentors, buddies, peer tutors, or members of learning teams are awarded for the skills and self-knowledge demonstrated by the student rather than for the activity itself. That is an important distinction, which applies also to credits given for work- and community-based experiences: the reward is given for learning demonstrated and recorded.

The development of skills and knowledge

Knowledge is what universities trade in. It is our claim to status and money. Intellectual vigour brings personal reward and advancement to society. It is essential to personal, social and cultural survival. But it is not sufficient. Our acknowledged strength as universities is also our recognized weakness. Graduates who know a lot but can achieve little are of limited use to others and liable to personal frustration. Capability can be recognized in the skilful use of knowledge and the knowledgeable use of skills, for skills and knowledge are not separable in performance. Effective students, like effective teachers, employ a range of personal skills in developing and using knowledge. Furthermore, knowledge itself, as a public discourse, grows exponentially and shifts identity. The graduate who has learned only information will soon forget most of it and find the rest has a short sell-by date. To further their personal and economic success, graduates must continue to learn with the skill and confidence a university education has given them.

The graduate sought by employers is actually not very different from the undergraduate teachers value. Universities who wish to encourage students to continue learning and to turn knowledge into action need to ensure that students experience courses which:

- have been designed by people who understand the relationship between knowledge and skills;
- focus on the central concepts and issues of a discipline and teach the intellectual strategies necessary to undertake further, independent learning;
- identify and promote the academic, professional and technical skills necessary to successfully practise and develop a discipline;
- explicate the way knowledge has shaped human perception and social reality, and encourage students to recognize the applications of knowledge to life beyond the university;
- demonstrate the evolutionary nature of knowledge and the dynamics of interdisciplinary discourse;
- identify and promote generic, transferable skills which are useful in a wide range of situations and contexts;
- provide documented strategies for the teaching and assessment of skills, including transferable skills, and opportunities for students to self-assess.

Are modular courses better at doing these? Not necessarily. Indeed, as suggested above, modularity's complexity of learning pathways requires considerable sophistication in both curriculum design and student support mechanisms to ensure coherent progression in the development of knowledge and skills. This is particularly apparent in the case of skills, whether they are the academic, technical or professional skills appropriate to a discipline or the general, transferable skills practised throughout an entire undergraduate career. In fact, those universities which have modular provision and are trying to introduce policies for transferable skills are finding it difficult to produce mapping mechanisms which will help staff and students to track progress, even with the help of a profiling system (Bonnett, Chapter 5, Chance, Chapter 6, and Jenkins, Scurry and Turner, Chapter 16 in this volume). The mapping, teaching and assessment of transferable skills is an art in its infancy. Expertise resides mainly in the United States and in the appraisal and training systems of industry and business, though there are interesting developments in the NVQ/GNVQ system, building on BTEC's experience in core skills.

If the integration of skills and knowledge appears to be more apparent in modular courses than in linear courses that is probably because modular courses are, as yet, more common in universities which were formerly polytechnics with a history of professional and vocational expertise. There is no reason in principle why modular courses should have a premium on skills.

Modular systems are advantaged in their ability to promote interdisciplinary connections through combinations of modules and dedicated interdisciplinary units of study. Students can also opt into the modules which stress the practical applications of study through case study, project work and work-experience, or modules which centre on transferable skills such as information technology, financial management, and modern foreign languages (Williams and Horobin, Chapter 8 in this volume).

Understanding the nature of work

Although many academic staff would disagree with the proposition that a university has an obligation to prepare all its graduates for working life, most students and employers welcome the idea. It is still possible for many young people to leave university in their early 20s without any formal experience of work or any sense of personal career development; yet a work-related curriculum is not a luxury. The country's future depends upon the skills and preparedness of tomorrow's leaders and managers; individual futures, too. Most graduates seek work, many find jobs for which they have had no formal preparation, many are ill-prepared and choose poorly. Universities which seriously seek to develop a work-related curriculum are characterized by the following indicators:

- opportunities for a range of credited work-based experiences, within and beyond professional and vocational courses;
- policy and practice for the development of skills (see above);
- courses which use the materials of working life for study and critical reflection;
- a supportive programme of career education, guidance and planning;
- a strong network of employers who play a variety of roles: assessors and examiners, course consultants, work-place mentors, voluntary tutors, course evaluators, resourcers, partners in curriculum design and delivery.

Modular provision would seem to improve the options for the middle three of those, though the design parameters are more complex, but it can widen the opportunities for ensuring the first and last items.

Such is the hermetic, self-referencing tendency of disciplines, that all universities find it hard to accommodate the career needs of students who are not engaged on study leading directly to a profession, other than through a central guidance service. Modular degree programmes can, however, more readily accommodate work-based learning experiences, whether related to academic disciplines (offering students of English work-experience in publishing companies, for instance) or extra-disciplinary (negotiated through learning contracts, as described by Gaskell, Brookes and Brierley, Chapter 12, in this volume, a scheme closely allied to those developed through the Work-based Learning for Academic Credit project [Learning from Experience Trust, 1993]).

Design issues for extracurricular work-based learning (where 'work' is used in its broadest sense to include community activities and university in-house activities) include the questions of how to credit learning which cannot be observed or which is unexpected (usually through a portfolio/

reflective journal/external commentary arrangement), the level(s) at which to credit the learning, and the ways in which the learning can be contextualized and used beyond the experience itself (usually through seminars and presentations which require students to consciously make connections).

Managerial requirements for the university centre on the infrastructure needed for placing and supporting students in work environments at a time of increasing demand on employers, the way in which resources are allocated to extra-disciplinary work-experience, and the academics who will validate the learning which occurs. Significantly, a number of universities moving towards a concept of a 'core' or 'entitlement' curriculum for undergraduates are beginning to express the rights of students to work-experience opportunities, whatever the nature of the academic studies – though the logistics of delivery are formidable. There are ways forward, however. The University of Coventry, for example, operates a Bureau for Employment of Students, managed by students themselves, who receive modular credit for the service they provide.

The involvement of employers (in its broadest definition of the whole range of people and organizations involved in working life, including voluntary and community organizations and trade unions) is critical in developing an outward-looking culture for universities. Capability is best developed in a university which shares in the creativity and everyday realities of society as a whole, and universities which offer modular programmes are particularly well placed to involve employers in a wide variety of roles beyond the provision of workplacements.

The 'Partnership Degree' is a state-of-the-art example. A university is asked to design and deliver a customized degree course in partnership with a company or group of companies. The employer identifies the expected outcomes for its employees and negotiates with the university about the learning experiences and the evidence required. The university ensures the programme is of degree standard and provides teaching input, with the other partner supplying technical expertise and workplace mentors. Mode of attendance is negotiated for individual students (employees) and so is the most suitable programme. Learning can be a mixture of class-based teaching, in-company research, work-based learning, intensive study weekends and distance/self-supported learning. The 'Partnership Degree' catches in its hands a whole set of developmental issues such as CATS, APEL, NVQ, learning contracts and work-based assessment: it cannot be delivered effectively other than through a modular arrangement. When universities can expect less funding from student fees and must generate more income from external sources, their ability to provide customized, flexible accreditation arrangements for students who are also workers may be essential.

Modularity, then, encourages work-related curricula and has the flexibility to respond to different clients with different needs. Depending upon the degree of latitude allowed by modular regulations, students can construct a coherent programme of academic and work-related experiences, backed up by targeted skills development and career planning, during which they will learn from people other than academics and significantly improve their chances in finding work.

Profiling and records of achievement

Recording one's own achievements (profiling) is an integral part of self-management, involving the collection of evidence, reflection on learning, recording of achievement and planning of future learning. While a final record of achievement is a useful summary document which may help a graduate find a first job, the process of self-understanding and communication encouraged by profiling is a requirement for lifelong learning and career development. Moreover, as university provision becomes more complex to negotiate, profiling is coming to be recognized as the most significant recent development in learner support systems.

The Enterprise in Higher Education programme has encouraged widespread piloting of profiling. Enterprise literature is now rich in examples (see, for example, Leicester University/Employment Department, 1994). This book contains several illustrations. Those who have been promoting profiling in higher education recognize that the questions have changed over time from 'Why profile' to 'How is profiling best achieved?'. The issue is not now whether university courses can develop profiling – they can (Pope, Chapter 7 in this volume) – but whether a university can guarantee equitable profiling for all undergraduate students within a unified but not uniform system (Jenkins, Scurry and Turner, Chapter 16 in this volume). This challenge is timely. More students from more varied backgrounds with more varied needs and goals are entering a higher education system of diversifying modes of learning and credit-transfer arrangements. It is easy to get lost, to lose identity, to make bad choices. Yet the modular programmes which so clearly need a profiling framework to guide students through complex learning experiences are the most difficult to organize and monitor.

My own university is one of the leaders in the field of profiling. After two years of piloting and consultation, a set of student entitlements has been agreed. They are not surprising in content but they have serious planning and resource consequences which other universities will recognize. Here is the entitlement statement:

The university should guarantee through review and validation processes that the following entitlements are being delivered.

Towards the beginning of his or her undergraduate experience, a student should be given opportunities to:

1. orient himself or herself to the processes of higher education in the university;
2. understand university and course/field-based procedures for profiling;
3. audit the skills, knowledges, abilities and experiences he or she has on entry;
4. understand the required learning outcomes of his or her chosen courses/fields;

5. identify personal learning needs and be advised of means of meeting those needs.

During the undergraduate programme, a student should be given opportunities to:

1. reflect upon and record the ways in which his or her personal learning develops;
2. create a learning record which includes unanticipated learning outcomes;
3. reflect upon and record knowledge, skills and learning experiences gained outside the academic curriculum;
4. receive clear feedback on his or her academic performance;
5. discuss academic progress and future learning needs with tutors;
6. receive support and guidance in gathering and organizing a portfolio of evidence of major achievements while at university;
7. receive support and advice in planning a future career.

Towards the end of the undergraduate programme a student should be given opportunities to:

1. receive support and guidance in reflecting upon and recording the skills, knowledge and achievement demonstrated while at university;
2. receive support and guidance in creating a final record of achievement;
3. receive from the university an academic transcript which identifies the knowledge and skills he or she has demonstrated;
4. receive support in using the final record and portfolio for purposes of career planning and interviews.

Our solution is to define the frameworks of entitlements for the modular course as a whole, but to place the responsibility for delivering the entitlement on individual schools, supported by university resources. Within those schools individual courses can meet some of the entitlements through methods suitable to their culture of learning – professional practice diaries, learning logs, reflective essays, learning contracts, peer-tutoring, self-assessment questionnaires and so on. Some courses (particularly those leading to a professional qualification, as in heath care and education) can provide most of the entitlements. The rest must be met by a combination of central services and personal tutors – and there's the rub. Personal tutor systems throughout higher education are strained or collapsed, the role of personal tutor is rarely timetabled, supported by training, or rewarded. We are now looking very carefully at the role and resourcing of personal tutors within the university. The requirement of providing good learner support to students on a modular course has led us towards profiling and that has, in its turn, forced us to confront the realities of personal support in a period of diminished funding. All choices for reallocating resources are hard – dedicated tutors and extra teaching for others, less direct teaching and more learning support, harder work and tighter job descriptions for all, redirection of resources from central services. Yet, if we believe in the centrality of the student experience and the systematic development and recording of knowledge and skills, we have no choice but to commit resources to profiling. Profiling cannot be undertaken half-heartedly or as an added extra: it is too important. The furtherance of capability, unfortunately, costs.

Before and after – lifelong learning and modularity

People who go to university usually leave shortly afterwards. Full-time university education normally takes up less than a thirteenth of a full working life and about a quarter of formal education. Most students come to us from schools, colleges or workplaces, stay a while, and leave for training or work in a world where the present is difficult and the future uncertain, where they will struggle to come to terms with the experience of rapid social and technological change. 'Lifelong learning' has become a necessary cliché and few academics, if any, believe that university provides the fuel to last the journey: all we can do is teach people to drive on their own. Yet not all academics understand the nature of the education and training opportunities that surround the university, or the extent to which universities are taking down their walls.

The education system which now precedes higher education would be unrecognizable to a teacher from 1960 and surprising to one from 1980. The system of accreditation operating in the world of work would be startling to a manager from 1985 and is still mysterious to most of them in 1994. Burke and Carey (Chapter 3 in this volume) outline the significant changes that have taken place in 14–19 education during the last decade, including the rising and falling fortunes of modularity. Modular A levels and GNVQ are set to impact with increasing force on higher education, not just in the potentially confusing portfolios of units of credit applicants will bring and the need for academics to unpack and interpret their content. Universities also need to recognize the expectations of students used to modular arrangements, clear learning outcomes, core skills, active learning methodologies and records of achievement. Moreover, institutions experimenting with modularity can learn a lot from those schools and colleges with over ten years of experience. For instance, in 1992 the Modular Information Network produced a set of principles for a modular approach to the curriculum (MIN,1992) which carry considerable meaning for higher education.

A module:

must have explicit aims;

must specify intended outcomes;

must specify, where appropriate, any prior learning which is required;

will make clear the methods of learning and the context in which the learning activities take place;

should provide for differentiated learning experience;

may be subject-specific, occupation-specific, cross-curricular, or a combination of these.

A programme of learning:

should have a clearly defined set of governing criteria;

should provide entry points based on previous learning experience and exit points consistent with future aspirations;

may be composed of modules of a variety of types;

must provide individual students with a balanced, progressive and coherent learning experience;

may incorporate modules which also appear in other programmes;

must be sufficiently flexible to meet the changing needs and aspirations of students.

Assessment in modules:

should be in relation to outcomes made explicit to students, staff and employers;

should be based upon a range of strategies through which a student can demonstrate what he or she knows, understands or can do;

should be based upon a range of evidence appropriate to the activity;

should include review and reflection, and lead to the identification of future goals and targets;

should facilitate the formative recording of achievement;

should be supported by appropriate quality assurance;

should enable students to gain credits for their attainments.

A university which achieved these criteria would satisfy most quality assurance investigations. The systems of modular accreditation operating pre-university are, however, more than models of good practice or features to be borne in mind when welcoming new undergraduates, for with the introduction of the General National Vocational Qualifications (GNVQs) and the parent system National Vocational Qualifications (NVQs), the university's control of its own curriculum is challenged. NVQ and GNVQ are about *competence*. Competence is not the same as capability, but it is allied. In G/NVQ competence refers to the ability to perform to predefined standards drawn from the realities of working life. Capability is a broader concept, involving personal development and intellectual ability, but the measurement of what people can *do* is a direct implication of defining a person's overall capability. It is therefore worth exploring some of the potential consequences of G/NVQ for universities, and asking how far those universities opening modular programmes can maintain their integrity within a national system of accreditation that is modular in a different sense to that operating within higher education.

NVQs and GNVQs are the major means for assessing the ability of people at work (or, in the case of GNVQ, for those going into work). They are designed to cover all sectors of the workforce at all levels of performance; they are unit-based and are derived from national standards of performance determined by professional and other lead bodies. The system is still in process of development and the higher levels of NVQ (and possibly GNVQ) are as yet only sketched in – but NVQ and GNVQ are here for the foreseeable future and will change what we teach, how we teach and how we assess.

In the short term the main effect will be on admissions tutors as more of the population have NVQ and GNVQ certification. If, or more likely when, GNVQ moves beyond level 3 most professional/vocational courses will be affected because standards, outcomes and assessment criteria may be largely determined by outside agencies. Furthermore, students on work placements may ask for NVQ assessment, which means that academic staff have to be qualified NVQ assessors. A number of universities are in fact already training academic staff to be NVQ assessors and verifiers. Eventually all professional and vocational degrees will have to take account of national standards at levels 4 and 5 (undergraduate and postgraduate equivalent). University courses which do not take account of these will be disadvantaged in recruiting students and may not receive external accreditation. Some universities are already looking to form consortia and work with professional and other lead bodies to act as NVQ centres – so they can certificate their students and also people who work outside the university, including the offer of an 'aftercare NVQ service' to their own alumni. If these consortia are successful, they will lead the market.

The effect of a fully-formed NVQ system of unit accreditation will also undoubtedly impact on credit accumulation and transfer arrangements between universities and industry and may well change the balance between full-time degrees and part-time, work-based degrees. G/NVQ will impact mainly on professional and vocational courses, but in the longer term, all courses may be affected to some extent. NVQ's stress on unit-based accreditation, work-related skills (including core skills), demonstrated competences and a lifelong record of learning may over time help to shift the emphasis and justifications of 'academic' courses.

Universities have had little involvement so far in helping NCVQ shape the nature of the NVQ system, and limited involvement with professional bodies in determining national standards. A united response is clearly required from the university sector but in the end it will be academics working with professional bodies who will have to take the NVQ/HE relationship forward.

Whether one agrees with the system or not, it is here and forces universities to adopt a position. The kind of capability universities can best develop in its students is more widely, more liberally defined than the competences of G/NVQ, yet G/NVQ has many attractive features, not least in making possible the kind of credit accumulation and transfer arrangements only previously dreamed of. What kind of questions should universities be asking, then, to respond to and, hopefully, shape the future of G/NVQ in relation to higher education? They probably need to include the following.

- G/NVQ is not a perfect system, in intention, design or mode of delivery. It is as yet too complicated, too compartmentalized and insufficiently aware of the importance of the theoretical and strategic elements of effective performance. By what mechanisms can university curriculum designers be centrally involved in the evolution of GNVQ and NVQ at the upper levels?

- What is the relation of a GNVQ unit to an HE module?
- What is the relation of an NVQ unit to a module?
- What is the relation between a GNVQ unit and an NVQ unit?
- What are the relationships between modules in different universities?
- How can a credit framework be established which will allow efficient incorporation of NVQ qualifications into degrees and long/short courses and what are the implications for the way universities design and offer programmes?
- How far can universities accommodate the detachment of credit from process (credit is given in NVQ for performance to standard, irrespective of how, where or when the performance was learned) and what opportunities does such a mechanism offer for the crediting of learning which takes place outside academic courses?
- How can knowledge and performance be successfully integrated to meet the functional requirements of industry and the traditional liberal/ humanist, critical, exploratory agenda of universities?
- How can the broader aspirations, diversified options and personal aspirations of students within a given degree programme embed the more tightly defined competences of NVQ based upon functional analyses of performance in specific work contexts?
- To what extent can universities act as assessment centres for GNVQ and NVQ within and beyond the university population and therefore to what extent will university staff themselves need NVQ qualifications in order to assess and verify?
- What will be the exact nature of the partnerships between academics and employers in design, teaching or mentoring, assessment and quality control – when and how will responsibilities be divided or shared?

Modular courses with clear learning outcomes, core skills development and work-related learning supported by profiling are far better placed to interact intelligently with the modular nature of the NVQ system than are linear, subject-based courses. Opportunities for credit exemption and transfer are becoming increasingly bound up not only with modularity but with particular kinds of modular delivery. The National Institute of Adult Continuing Education (NIACE), for example, explicitly connect structure and style in their principles for credit arrangements. They describe (NIACE, 1993) the necessary requirements for higher education as

...a coherent national credit framework for post school education and training to provide the underpinning for all qualifications, whether work based or academic, at all levels from basic education to post graduate education. This will:

- enable individuals to acquire, accumulate and transfer credit between institutions and programmes

- recognise a broad range of achievement, in small stages
- be based on explicit statements of learning outcomes
- build coherence around individually negotiated agreements
- use a variety of assessment approaches
- make assessment accessible
- provide open entry to higher education at multiple levels.

The interface between academic life and working life is complex and becoming more so as the need grows for sophisticated credit transfer arrangements of a modular kind. We cannot, of course, only prepare graduates to work within the United Kingdom. There is no space here to explore the modular systems of education and training developing in Europe and the rest of the world and this chapter will be very dusty indeed when, if ever, an international credit accumulation and transfer system which involves both education and training is in place (though the Employment Department's *A Higher Education Credit Accumulation and Transfer Strategy for Europe* (University of Teesside/Employment Department, 1992) and the European Community's *Euroqualification Info* bulletins make interesting reading). Nevertheless, British graduates with clearly described achievements which include transferable skills and a portfolio of modules which demonstrate work-related abilities will be better placed than those who have none.

Capability and the core curriculum

A modular system is by nature dynamic, continually rebalancing its elements, adding, jettisoning, repositioning, as new areas of knowledge and new external agendas come into play. Yet curriculum change, modular or otherwise, is by nature incremental – the original ground plan and early foundations act as (often unrecognized) design constraints on later architects; new parts are added – extension, annexes, bridges – each with its own rationale, well-designed in itself, each contributing to an increasingly complicated structure. The purposes of higher education, too, can be perceived as contradictory by academics who are called upon to provide 'a general educational experience of intrinsic worth ... a preparation for knowledge creation ... specific vocational preparation ... preparation for general employment' while they are balancing teaching, pastoral care, scholarship, research, administration, management and career politics (Newcastle University/Employment Department, 1993). The likelihood of incrementally achieving a well-designed, coherent curriculum to suit all students is low and the dangers are greater for a modular scheme, for 'dynamic' can easily become 'unstable'.

The argument for capability, however, seems to be an argument for a particular kind of student experience (based on skills development as well as knowledge, the growth of learner autonomy, extracurricular and work-based learning), as a particular kind of methodology (active learning, problem solving, profiling) and a particular set of attributes which define a desirable graduate.

A common set of learning outcomes informed by a common set of teaching and learning methods and inspired by a common set of educational principles, is one definition of a core curriculum. It is not surprising, therefore, that British universities have begun to look at the American experience of core curricula, asking how far that experience can be translated into a different culture and whether the notion of a core curriculum offers a design solution to a potentially incoherent undergraduate programme.

A core curriculum can be defined in a number of ways and delivered by a number of methods. The 'core' may be a core of knowledge the university feels all students should encounter (50 books that changed the world, Aristotle to Ariosto in one term), a range of disciplines one should be familiar with (compulsory foundation science, an introduction to economics), a set of experiences students should undertake (working in the community), a range of abilities (using information technology, working in teams), or a list of dispositions, attitudes and values (citizenship, multi-cultural awareness). Usually a core is defined as a mixture of knowledge, experiences, abilities and values and it often represents an uneasy compromise between powerful lobby groups within the university. Those universities which have developed their cores over a decade or more (such as Denver, Alverno or Harvard, whose deliberations are over a century old) testify to the struggles and triumphs of an intellectual community debating its own identity. British universities, mainly because of their high entry requirements, the autonomy of disciplines, a suspicion of overt social engineering and a residual belief that different students have different needs, have shown less interest in a core curriculum, but that is changing. Roper (Chapter 17 in this volume) offers a personal view of the common principles or entitlements which might underlie a student experience.

A coherent core curriculum based upon the concept of capability can indeed operate within a modular setting, though, to my knowledge, it does not so operate in any British university other than as a desire to ensure certain common elements such as the development of transferable skills or the opportunity to gain credit for work experience. There are several design options, requiring different levels of cross-university agreement and involving different degrees of administrative pain. For example:

- A set of student entitlements or learning requirements (depending on the degree of compulsion involved) which can be delivered by all courses in their own way (eg, the right for students to be made aware of career options arising from the knowledge and skills gained in a course). The onus is on course teams to demonstrate where and how the entitlements are available.
- A set of unattached compulsory modules for all students (eg, a profiling module or a work-based module).
- A set of core modules within each course which guarantees certain kinds of learning takes place (eg, how to make group presentations in subject x).
- A set of required skills or abilities which all courses must develop within a common descriptive and assessment framework (eg, the transferable

skills model developed by Sheffield University, currently used in a *voluntary* way by some courses).

- A set of required learning experiences (rules of study) which are built into a variety of accessible modules. The student has to negotiate a curriculum which meets the requirements (eg, to reach a certain level of skill in using information technology).
- A set of short module courses which make up a core curriculum and from which a student negotiates a balanced programme which takes prior learning into account.
- A set of foundation or learning-support modules designed to enable students to reach a level of performance which the university believes all graduates should attain (eg, in numeracy, academic English, information-handling skills, or a modern foreign language).

One suspects that the British core curriculum is in fact being developed incrementally to acclimatize the more diverse range of students entering higher education and in response to the employability requirements of graduates. If the present directions are followed through, the British core curriculum will not be defined in epistemological or cultural terms but in the language of abilities, skills and entitlements. Modular courses have a more difficult territory to control but have more strategies to play with, more ways to win and more opportunities to get it wrong.

Conclusion

This chapter has considered some of the relationships between 'capability' and 'modularity'. Although they are, like all educational concepts, ambiguous terms in an unresolved equation and are both rather too young in years to offer substantial evidence of success, there is perhaps sufficient identity in the idea of 'capability' and sufficient commonality in the practice of modular universities to make some reasonable connections.

My view is that the nature of the undergraduate curriculum, for better or worse, is changing under pressure – new 'clients' and more of them, new funding regimes, externally generated quality audit and assurance criteria, industry-led qualifications. The autonomy of academic life is squeezed between student demand and public accountability and that may be no bad thing if it means we have to demonstrate our own capability as teachers. I also believe that universities operating modular schemes can certainly offer a curriculum which encourages students to become independent learners and skilful actors, more so than the linear courses offered within traditional degree programmes, and are particularly well placed to cope with the vital interconnections between learning at university and learning at work. However, it also seems clear to me that the elements which could combine to make a truly coherent 'capability curriculum' are as yet present only in patches, and that the examples of practice and exploration described in this book and elsewhere need to be fully integrated in modular schemes which are explicitly designed to meet the needs of those who will sustain and develop our society.

It may be objected that all this talk of capability is social engineering. It is. All education is social engineering and we should not pretend that 'traditional' (ie nineteenth-century) liberal humanism is otherwise. We can call 'capability' the New Vocationalism but we can equally well call it the New Liberalism, based on helping students to understand and act upon the world in skilful, intelligent ways. The issue is contentious and we ought not to fudge it. Their careers and our pensions depend upon it.

References

Eggins, H (ed.) (1992) *Art Graduates: Their skills and their employment*, London: Falmer Press. (The chapter 'Classification and Models for Transferable Skills' by D Bradshaw is particularly useful.)

Learning from Experience Trust (1993) *Work Based Learning for Academic Credit*, London: HMSO.

Leicester University/Employment Department (1994) *Bibliography No 8, Profiling and Records of Achievement in Higher Education*, Leicester: Leicester University Enterprise Learning Initiative.

Modular Information Network (1992) *Principle for a Modular Approach to the Curriculum*, Weybridge: Surrey TVU Unit.

Newcastle University/Employment Department (1993) *Assessment Issues in Higher Education*, London: DoE.

NIACE (1993) *An Adult Higher Education* (Policy discussion paper), Leicester: NIACE.

University of Teesside/Employment Department (1992) *A Higher Education Credit Accumulation and Transfer Strategy for Europe*, London: DoE.

Chapter 3

Modular Developments in Secondary and Further Education: Their Implications for Higher Education

Peter Burke and Adrian Carey

Introduction

One of the central concerns in British school education throughout the 1980s has been the need to raise standards, although as yet there seems to be no commonly agreed definition of precisely what those standards are. The introduction of the new GCSE examining system in 1988 is frequently alleged to have brought in its wake a decline in standards compared with the old GCE Ordinary Level examination. This is somewhat paradoxical since under the norm-referenced O Level system (and the same is true for A Level) the standards were never articulated, so that the meaning of grades in terms of the knowledge, skills and understanding required to attain them was impenetrable, especially to the candidates. GCSE represented the first attempt in a UK public examining system to produce criteria to define the meaning of the grades. Similarly the National Curriculum has also tried to define levels of performance against which to assess students at key stages in their schooling.

Underpinning the belief that standards need to be raised is the consequent and more important assumption that students must be underachieving. Indeed, one of the principal reasons cited by Sir Keith Joseph for introducing GCSE was that students would be given clear targets to aim for, in terms of what they should 'know, understand and can do', in order to raise their level of achievement. It is in this context – the desire to provide opportunities for students of all abilities to do better and fulfil their potential – that the debate about modularity in the 14–19 age range should be conducted.

Ten years of modularity: a review of the issues and outcomes

The publication of the Inner London Education Authority's report *Improving Secondary Schools* (ILEA, 1984) was the stimulus for much of the interest that was to follow in modular curriculum developments. In the report, David Hargreaves argued for a fundamental restructuring of the curriculum in order to provide students with the opportunity to apply knowledge to practical situations and to develop personal and social skills. It found that the existing curriculum and examination system promoted self-expression through writing at the expense of other aspects of achievement, and that many students were neither motivated by nor committed to the current approach. At the same time Bob Moon, then the head of Peers School, Oxford, was expressing anxieties about what he called 'the deference curriculum', which was common to most secondary schools and in which some subjects were given a higher status than others because of their supposed greater academic worth. This divided curriculum was reflected in the subject choices of the abler and less able students.

For both Moon and Hargreaves the solution to these problems was to be found in modules. Modules would allow all students at Peers School to study science, humanities and creative arts, and would enhance student motivation and commitment by providing clear short-term learning targets. Support for this thesis came from the Technical and Vocational Education Initiative (TVEI), which promoted new 'subjects' such as business studies, technology (especially information technology) and electronics to full curriculum status, and required students to show problem-solving and practical skills. This could only be accomplished in an already overcrowded curriculum through the construction of short modular courses, many of which were to be developed within the embryonic GCSE system. In reaching this conclusion incidentally, they had anticipated by some ten years the outcomes of the Dearing 1993 (SCAA, 1994) review of the British National Curriculum structure.

It was in this early work that much of the agenda for the modular debate was set. Arguments about proliferation of syllabus provision, the dangers of curriculum incoherence and the need for a consistent assessment standard from the first to the last module in a course tended to obscure what was seen to be the fundamental argument in favour of modules, namely *that they provide an effective system for managing learning to the advantage of all students.* In order to take advantage of this possibility, a set of ground rules began to emerge to underpin modular developments and to provide guidance for course developers. It became generally accepted that a module should be defined as a short unit of learning which could be linked to other modules to form a coherent programme, and that each module:

- should have clearly defined aims and expected outcomes;
- should specify content (in terms of knowledge, skills and understanding);
- should refer to appropriate teaching and learning styles; and

- should explain the method(s) of assessment to be used.

While all this provided a technical framework for modular developments, especially within GCSE, it was the range and quality of curriculum delivery and learning benefits which were beginning to emerge which really attracted growing interest. Students were able to become more centrally involved in making decisions about their own learning. The short-term nature of the module and the clearly specified outcomes compared very favourably with the traditional two-year course with obscure objectives and terminal testing. Regular review of progress towards the outcomes with the teacher throughout the module and the immediacy of the assessment integrated with the learning process, proved an effective basis for planning the next steps in learning, thereby improving progression. Above all, however, reports of increased student motivation leading to enhanced performance across the ability range were widespread.

Although most early initiatives were focused on the 14–16 age range, there was also a developing interest in taking the outcomes forward into the post-16 phase, in order to provide continuity of experience for students and to take advantage of the perceived benefits. The introduction of the TVEI Extension Programme also played a key part in promoting the need for curriculum planning on a 14–19 basis. The University of Cambridge Local Examinations Syndicate was early into the field with its A Level 'Modular Bank', and the Wessex A Level pilot scheme (Rainbow, 1987) was developed in 1987 by a number of LEAs in the south-west, and was certificated by the Associated Examining Board. In addition, the vocational examining boards (BTEC, RSA and CGLI) were also offering a number of modular courses.

The flood of new development was somewhat stemmed however at the end of the 1980s when the Secondary Examinations Council (SEC) and its successor the School Examinations and Assessment Council (SEAC) introduced new regulations for the development and assessment of GCSE and A Level examinations, restricting the permitted amount of coursework and stressing the importance of a terminal examination, both of which were antipathetic to the principles of modularity and active student involvement in the learning process.

Interest in the modular curriculum has remained high however and recently pressure for more flexibility in course design and delivery and in assessment has come about from the introduction of the General National Vocational Qualification (GNVQ), which the government wishes to have parity of esteem with A Level in terms of access to higher education and entry into employment. GNVQ offers unit-based programmes of study with a core skills component. Assessment is mainly through the compilation of portfolios of evidence, managed by the student. The prospect of post-16 students studying a combination of A Level and GNVQ has therefore put modules firmly back on the agenda, and some GCSE boards are now endeavouring to develop modular syllabuses which will provide a common curriculum pathway to separate certificate destinations.

In any event the debate has moved on since the ILEA report and the focus is now on the 14–19 age range, with the need to improve access to higher education and eliminate the academic/vocational divide as the most urgent issues. So in 1994, as in 1984, modules are seen to offer a way forward, and initiatives such as the GLOSCAT (Gloucestershire College of Arts and Technology, 1992) Project and the Liverpool Enrichment Programme (University of Liverpool, 1991) provide useful case studies for others to learn from.

While all this has been going on another significant and related concept has also gained ground. Following a modular programme offers students the opportunity to gain credit for their achievements as they complete each module. The Further Education Unit (FEU) has taken the concept of 'credit' a stage further and piloted a model – the so-called CAT Framework – within which credits can be accumulated and transferred within and between courses and institutions. The benefits of such a flexible arrangement are described in the FEU's discussion document *A Basis for Credit?* (FEU, 1992).

Another key player in the recent past has been the increasingly influential Modular Information Network (MIN), originally set up in the mid-1980s to provide a forum for innovation and modular course development but now operating as a support agent for the development of flexible modular and credit-based courses for the whole 14–19 curriculum. MIN's most significant contribution has been the publication of the *Principles for a Modular Approach to the Curriculum* (MIN, 1992), which set out the principles under five areas:

- mechanisms for ensuring breadth and balance;
- flexibility in constructing learning programmes;
- integration across the curriculum;
- feedback, for recording achievement and action planning;
- the linking of academic and vocational courses

with case studies to exemplify and illustrate each area.

Implications of the 14–19 experience for higher education

Modularity has done much to change attitudes to learning and particularly to develop the role of the student in managing the learning. What has happened is that students have become more effective learners not only because dividing the curriculum up into what Henry Macintosh describes as 'manageable chunks' (Macintosh, 1992) is perfectly natural and reflects the way we tend to learn and helps to demystify the assessment process, but also because the curriculum experience has been enriched by the incorporation of complementary processes such as action planning, recording of achievement, portfolio reviews, supported self-study and resource-based learning. Flexible approaches to teaching and learning such as these have encouraged students to produce a wide variety of forms of evidence of achievement thereby helping to reduce the over-emphasis on continuous prose to which Hargreaves referred. As a consequence the role of the teacher has also undergone a significant shift away from the traditional didactic style to a more supportive, collaborative one. In short, modularity has done much to promote Foundation Target 4 (education and training to develop self-reliance, flexibility and breadth), which is widely regarded as the most important of the government's National Training and Education Targets (NTETs).

Foundation Target 4 is concerned with nurturing those skills and attitudes which will empower individual students to take charge of their own learning and consequently pave the way for the development of the Lifetime Learning Targets. The concept of 'lifetime learning' suggests that people will wish to continue learning throughout their lives. If this is the case, then higher education institutions will need to respond and organize themselves in such a way as to give this continued access to education. This will require two things: flexible course structures and delivery systems; and the development in learners of appropriate skills and qualities.

Flexible course structures and delivery systems will permit each student to construct a bespoke programme of study, based on modules, to suit their needs and interests, and out of which they can gain credits towards a variety of qualifications which will enable them to progress to another tier of education or to another sphere of employment/training. The adoption of an APL (Accreditation of Prior Learning) model will also enable previous learning and achievement to be recognized, wherever or however it occurred. Access to this curriculum will also be enhanced by the introduction of teaching and learning styles such as flexible learning, open learning, supported self-study, distance learning programmes and 'drop-in' workshops which place the learner at the centre of the process. The adoption of a more appropriate assessment model based on the assembly of portfolios of evidence will also be an important feature in support of a more flexible curriculum.

The development in learners of appropriate skills and qualities will enable them to exploit these flexible systems. Students will need to become independent learners, empowered to take charge of their own learning, able to review and assess past progress and achievement, identify future learning needs and goals, negotiate the appropriate learning opportunities to meet those needs, manage their own learning, objectively assess and evaluate their own performance, and transfer key skills to a variety of different contexts. To support the development of these skills and attitudes they will need to employ the processes of individual action planning and recording of achievement which underpin the concept of the 'lifetime learner'.

Students and teachers in schools and colleges who have embarked on modular courses have already made this leap forward. In an era of wider access and course franchising in higher education, modularity can also enable universities to offer flexible, high quality courses in an economic way. As the MIN case study *Modularity and Effective Learning* records:

Modularity is cost-effective in many ways. Students' motivation and success are fostered not just by shorter-term goals and frequent feedback, but also by regular opportunity to re-direct programmes according to developing interest and skill. Modules allow for more joint teaching on closely related programmes. They make it easier to combine full-time and part-time students and adult returners....They encourage explicit learning targets and processes, thus increasing the likelihood that students, by controlling it more, will complete and succeed in their work. Cost-effectiveness means making the most effective use of the most costly and valuable resource: teachers. Students can – and do – acquire much of their knowledge from other resources; modern technology makes this increasingly possible and stimulating. Teachers' special abilities lie in designing learning activities; in motivating and stimulating students; in developing their learning skills; in helping them to reflect on, make meaning of and unify their learning; in assuring assessment; and in offering guidance and direction. Modular courses provide a framework in which these roles are easier to identify and fulfil, just as they make such roles more important. The teacher's shift, from one who prepares lessons to one who prepares learning, is crucial. (Boothroyd, 1993)

This then is the challenge facing higher education over the next decade as the number of students going on to university continues to increase. It will require HE institutions to reconsider not only their courses, but also their management structures. Flexibility of curriculum delivery cannot be properly implemented in an institution in which the supremacy of 'subjects' remains unchanged and unchallenged. The experience from Peers School, albeit on a smaller scale, clearly illustrates this. It may also demand a wide ranging programme of staff development to enable tutors to introduce new teaching and learning styles and adopt a more supportive role. Most important of all perhaps will be the flexibility to award credit (and therefore exemption) at the point of entry into HE to students for their existing skills and knowledge.

References

Boothroyd, C (1993) *Modularity and Effective Learning*, Modular Information Network (MIN), Runnymede Centre, Chertsey Road, Addlestone, Weybridge, Surrey.

Further Education Unit (1992) *A Basis for Credit? Developing a post-16 credit accumulation and transfer framework – a paper for discussion*, London: FEU.

Gloucestershire College of Arts and Technology (1992) *The GLOSCAT Project*, Cheltenham, Gloucestershire.

Inner London Education Authority (1984) *Improving Secondary Schools*, London: ILEA.

Macintosh, H (1992) 'Trust in units', *Education* 14 August.

Modular Information Network (MIN) (1992) *Principles for a Modular Approach to the Curriculum*, Runnymede Centre, Chertsey Road, Addlestone, Weybridge, Surrey.

Rainbow, R (1987) *The Wessex Project – Modular Developments Post-16*, Holyrood Community School, Chard, Somerset.

School Curriculum and Assessment Authority (1994) *The National Curriculum and its Assessment: Final Report*, London: SCAA.

University of Liverpool (1991) *Developing Skills for a Working Life*, The University of Liverpool Curriculum Enrichment Programme.

Chapter 4

Modular Courses, Assessment and Student Capability

Marilyn Leask

Developing a modular degree programme

Over a three-year period, the first degree programmes at Bedford College of Higher Education were rewritten as modular degree programmes, partly in response to the national Credit and Accumulation Transfer Scheme (CATS), which eases student transfer between institutions, partly to widen student choice and partly to ensure more efficient use of resources. The courses affected included those for BA, BSc, BEd (primary) and BEd (secondary) degrees.

When the new modules were being devised, staff were encouraged to include a range of assessment strategies to suit the work the students were undertaking. There were, of course, certain constraints. The assessment for each module was to be equivalent to the production of a 2,500-word essay. Modules are designed to provide 30 hours of student/lecturer contact time and 70 hours 'non-contact' time. The modules are taught in two-hour blocks over one semester, ie a 15-week period, and the teaching year is divided into two semesters. The sizes of teaching groups vary from about 20 to 120 with some provision for personal tutorials on a one-to-one basis.

In this chapter, the results of a small-scale study reviewing staff and student experience with assessment on the modular programmes are discussed. Although the findings are context-specific, nevertheless a number of issues were raised which are worthy of consideration within the context of enhancing student capability through modular degree programmes. Quotations from students and staff are provided in the text but they are coded to provide anonymity.

Methodology

I collected data from students and staff using questionnaires and interviews. I also analysed course documentation. Open-ended interviews with a small number of staff and students were used initially to identify concerns that could be followed up through a questionnaire. Two groups of students on the new programmes completed questionnaires. The groups were unknown to each other as they came from different sites and different degree programmes. One group was in the second year and the other was in the first year. I administered questionnaires to students as they attended lectures so there was a high response rate from the sample groups. The questions were open-ended, again to allow the main areas of concern to be identified. A third group of students, from the last cohort on a non-modular degree, were asked to contrast their experiences of assessment (some assessed course work with end-of-year examinations) with those of their friends on the new modular degree.

Questionnaires coupled with selected in-depth interviews were used to collect data from staff. The sample included 60 students, and about 20 per cent of the staff who are significantly involved in teaching on modular degree programmes. The majority of these staff have also taught on traditional degree programmes.

Modular assessment: does it enhance student capability?

In seeking to answer the question above, I identified four main contexts through which modular assessment could be used to enhance student capability:

- where the assessment is used formatively, ie if students are able to use the assessments to improve the quality of future assignments;
- where a variety of forms of assessment is used – so that assessment is not narrowly focused on one aspect of performance – for example, the memorization of facts;
- where assessment is seen to be fair and relevant;
- where an overall assessment framework exists which is designed to ensure coherence and progression in student learning.

This is not a definitive list, nor are items listed in order of importance, but the four contexts provided a useful framework for the analysis of the data.

In order to identify central concerns about and the successes of modular assessment, students and staff were simply asked to identify any positive and any negative features of assessment within the modular system. I then used the framework provided by the four contexts to analyse the data. The results are as follows.

The formative use of assessment

More than half of both groups of students found the monitoring of their progress through modular assessment particularly helpful. As one student wrote: 'Assessment …gives an idea of how you are coping with the course and the results and expectations of the module are available at a time when help is of value' (1P,10). Many students thought that the continual monitoring provided by modular assessment improved attainment. The comment 'You can keep track of your progress. If you do badly in one assessment, you can pick up on the next assessment' (1P,9) incorporates the view expressed by a number of students. But about a quarter of the staff commented that because most assessments fall at the end of the module, opportunities for feedback to students are limited. Interestingly, none of the students made this comment and about a quarter of the Year 1 students specifically mentioned the positive help they'd had from tutorial staff. This may indicate that whilst staff see modules are discrete items, students see them as part of a larger process of learning.

Staff commented that the availability of assessment results early in a degree course was useful to students and that students used assessment methods as one criterion for the choice of modules. Two members of staff felt that the quality of student work improved as students were working more consistently throughout the year. Students who said that having to work continuously was an issue were divided in their views about whether this was a positive or a negative feature.

A couple of students commented that the modular system aids learning through investigation and they felt this consolidated their knowledge.

Variety of forms of assessment

Staff were urged to integrate a range of assessment strategies into the modular programmes. The CNAA documents (Burgess and Lee, 1989; CNAA 1989, 1990, 1992) were cited by some staff as being particularly helpful in providing examples of different approaches. (See Table 4.1)

Table 4.1 *A summary of the assessment methods used on courses*

Examples of the assessment methods used on courses:

- production of resource packs
- essays (usually on problematic education issues)
- analysis of school policy statements
- teaching experience plans and evaluation
- laboratory manual completion
- staff and peer assessment of seminar work
- display (using IT or visual aids)
- presentation of a sequence (dance or gym)
- formal examination (with a variety of types of question)
- short tests
- analysis of case studies
- group displays
- tests with viva
- seminar notes
- logs or diaries
- seen questions
- investigations
- practical assessments
- oral presentations

Note: The courses are modular and assessment for each module is the equivalent of a 2,500-word essay. There is also an action research project (about 10,000 words).

The experience reported by the students confirms that a variety of assessment strategies are used. All the Year 1 students had experienced at least three different types of assessment in the preceding semester, with the majority experiencing four or five. The assessments included essays, oral presentations, practical assessments, laboratory notes, portfolios of work, examinations. The Year 2 students (on a different degree programme) reported less variety of assessment in the preceding semester. All had experienced at least two forms of assessment (essay and examination) with many reporting three (the third being either oral assessment or practical assessment). This possibly suggests a fall back to more traditional forms of assessment although when their experience of earlier modules is taken into account, the forms of assessment mirror those for the Year 1 students. The analysis of course documentation for both groups indicates that the use of wide variety of assessment strategies is intended.

Some staff commented that assessment could tend to be 'bitty' and that there could be some loss of student capability in essay writing when other forms of assessment are used. A positive comment was that lecturers were able to match content with an appropriate assessment method.

Assessment is seen to be fair and relevant

A number of students made comments similar to the following one – that modular assessment 'makes the course far more interesting and learning becomes a pleasure' (1P,7). Others said the forms of assessment used encouraged students to read more widely rather than just to revise from notes for an examination. 'This [the research required] ensures that the student has an understanding of the topics' (2S,6). Unevenness of assessment between modules and unevenness of standard between lecturers were identified by a small number of students as areas of concern.

The second year group made quite strong statements about their preference for a modular system over a more traditional 'finals' system. Almost all students in this group said the modular system was fairer.

Student workloads

Complaints from students about the assessment workload on the modular degree were among the concerns which prompted this study. However, when students were faced with the option of the alternative system of examinations at the end of a year or two, they clearly considered that modular assessment had significant advantages in spite of the workload. One student summed up the views voiced by more than half of each student group:

'It [modular assessment] takes the pressure off'. Another commented that 'knowing what standard you were working to' was a positive feature of modular assessment.

A couple of students suggested that modular assessment was less demanding for students than traditional examinations – 'less self-discipline is needed to do well', one student suggested (1P,17). Another student made the point that there was 'no reason to retain any of the information after the module finishes' (2S,6). This point reflects staff concerns about the depth of coverage of a subject in a modular system where prerequisites for the taking of modules are kept to a minimum to allow for flexibility. Staff identified progression as a problem as students come with different academic backgrounds. There was also seen to be less scope for individual excellence and specialization.

'Bunching' of assessment was identified by more than half the students in each group and by more than half of the staff as being an issue of concern. The degree submissions do show that assessments are 'bunched' at the half-way mark (after seven weeks of two hours of lectures per week) and at the end of the module. Some staff and students commented that students need to be able to manage their time well.

Over assessment?

The third group of students, the last cohort of a non-modular degree, recognized the advantages of modular assessment, particularly the lack of final examinations and the relevance of assessment of current work. But they were unanimous in their concern about the level of work that they had seen those in the year below them having to undertake. Staff too have voiced the concern that students are 'over-assessed' within the modular scheme. This seems to happen simply because each module is assessed and although the assessment is meant to be the equivalent of a 2,500-word essay where a variety of methods are used, it can be difficult to quantify the work the students actually have to do.

The assessment framework

Staff saw a number of advantages of modular assessment in improving the quality of courses. Assessment could be seen as 'an integral part of teaching' (S2), one member of staff wrote. Others considered that modular assessment demands 'clear objectives' (S7) with the 'learning outcomes set out' (S8). One commented that the planning process was streamlined as 'fewer staff are involved in compilation of assessment' (S5), whilst another considered that 'careful planning and structuring of courses' was a positive demand of modular work.

Communication between different departments within the institution was *ad hoc* at lecturer level. This meant that strategies which staff devised and lessons which staff learnt from the implementation of the first phase of modularization were not necessarily communicated to those planning the following phases. One example is the assessment framework developed by one department in the first phase of modularization. Staff developing some BSc modules planned their assessment on the basis of three levels which roughly equate to the year of study – Level 1 focusing on acquisition of skills, Level 2 on synthesis of knowledge and Level 3 on interpretation. In anticipation of higher student numbers, staff decided to assess through examinations based on computer-marked multiple choice questions for Level 1. At Level 2 the assessment was planned to be about one-third multiple choice and two-thirds laboratory practical work; at Level 3 assessment included essay work and practical work. Staff marking loads were thus more controlled. Solutions to the problem of increased marking load for staff could have been recognized earlier.

Marking load

The phased introduction of a modular degree means that staff are cushioned from the full impact of the change for a couple of years. As a modular degree is progressively implemented, the marking load builds up. In the first year, only the marking from one cohort of students comes toward the end of the module; in the second year, the marking for two cohorts falls at the same time and by the third year, with three groups now on a modular programme, the volume of marking occurring at the same time could become a significant problem unless action is taken to avoid marking overload. Staff teaching loads in any one semester vary too, so that staff with heavy teaching loads in one semester could find themselves with an enormous marking load. The higher staff:student ratios of recent years exacerbate the problem and planning needs to take account of the issue. This raises a question about the desirability of a whole-institution policy on assessment.

Other issues

One interesting issue which staff raised, which does not relate directly to modular assessment but is worth mentioning in the context of enhancing student capability, is staff/student relationships. Some members of staff feel there is a loss in continuity of relationships on modular courses as students are no longer identifiable as being on one particular course. As this loss of identity may well have an impact on students' sense of self-worth and the formation of supportive student networks, the issue is worthy of considera-tion in the debate about modularity and the enhancement of student capability.

While few of the students made comments on the issue of progression in learning and the potential lack of coherence and depth in modular programmes, these concerns were expressed by some staff. These are clearly areas where work needs to be done.

Conclusion

Modular assessment is in a number of respects similar to continuous assessment and the benefits of enhanced student capability identified through this study are probably available to students on courses with traditional teaching structures which use continuous and varied assessment strategies. The problem of 'bunching' of assessment which is perhaps inevitable with modular degree programmes does need to be anticipated and actively managed by students and staff alike.

This case study, limited as it is in scope, raises a number of issues concerning modular assessment and the enhancement of student capability which those proceeding down the modular course route may wish to consider:

- Modular assessment can play a formative role thus enhancing student learning.
- Students need to be well organized and to be able to manage their time well.

- Students consider the system fairer than an examination system but steps should be taken to ensure similar standards between modules and lecturers.
- Modular assessment is generally perceived as relevant.
- A tendency to over-assessment may occur.
- An institutional assessment policy may enhance comparability and progression and ensure the sharing of good practice.
- The phasing of assessment needs to be planned to ease workloads. A constraint is that modules finish at the same time to allow changeover.
- There may be some cost in terms of specialization and depth if a wide choice of modules is permitted.
- Staff/student and student/student relationships may be affected.

If those planning modular courses take account of these points, they may be able to avoid some of the pitfalls that await the unwary treading the new ground of modular assessment and thus more easily reap the rewards of modularization.

References

Burgess, R and Lee, B (1989) *Good Practice in Assessment: Criteria and procedures for CNAA undergraduate courses*, Development Services Report 22, London: Council for National Academic Awards.

CNAA (1989) *How Shall We Assess Them?*, London: CNAA.

CNAA (1990) *Assessment in Schools: Implications for Teacher Education*, London: CNAA.

CNAA (1992) *Competence-based Approaches to Teacher Education: Viewpoints and Issues*, Project Report 33, London: CNAA.

SECTION B:
CORE MODULES AND CORE SKILLS

Chapter 5

The Integration of Core Personal Skills into a Tutorial System in Biological Sciences (Hons) Degrees

Linda Bonnett

Introduction

A traditional science department with an active research profile in a large civic university (14,000 students), the Department of Biochemistry and Molecular Biology at the University of Leeds has developed a modular undergraduate programme in line with institutional policy. This process, with its emphasis on outcomes, has raised awareness of issues of both content and delivery in teaching. At the same time, modularity generates concern about continuity and coherence in the experience of single and combined honours students in biochemistry and other biological and paramedical students taking biochemistry modules. Our researchers of international reputation are aware that in such rapidly advancing fields as molecular biology, biotechnology and genetic engineering, the knowledge base of graduates becomes dated quickly.

This must be true of other science subjects. During the negotiation of an industrial 'sandwich' element to our modular degree programme, dialogue with graduate employers has placed emphasis on the importance of personal and professional transferable skills for graduates accepting the challenge of employment in the twenty-first century in these, and any other, dynamic areas. It seems that developing student capability in core skills, equipping them to be adaptive and to use their knowledge base to fiunction as effective problem solvers and communicators – always an implicit aspect of undergraduate teaching – should be made explicit and given value.

Students are now arriving at university with some background of support for personal development from school: many have records of achievement, are aware of their personal skills and able to exhibit these on UCAS forms and at interview. We need to encourage students to continue developing these essential skills.

The department has supplied the customized biochemical contents of several biological degree schemes at Levels I and II, premodularization. Teaching has always comprised a clear knowledge-based lecture and practical programme supported by tutorial arrangements which consisted of a set number of timetabled, one-hour tutorials. Each year some 500 students were involved and delivery was by a number of tutors of varied biochemical expertise. An *ad hoc* arrangement was in place for tutorial content. There was some concern about the consistency of student experience and their perception of the relevance of this biochemistry, since student motivation was sometimes seen to be lacking. The fear was that this aspect might deteriorate under a modular structure. Modularization resulted in 12 second-year and three first-year biochemical modules. Varying numbers of these are applicable to 16 or more modular degree programmes – to a maximum of 400 students taking one module. In this context the core skills development of undergraduates attending biochemistry modules was considered.

The institutional staff development facilities and the Enterprise in Higher Education Initiative provide resources of which interested staff may take advantage for innovative curriculum development in core skills areas. The relative success of these activities among a small number of staff in the department led to the appointment, with support from the institutional Academic Development Fund, of a staff member with a specific brief to compile and implement a strategy for undergraduate 'core skills' development. Departmental discussions revealed a reluctance to devote an entire credit-bearing module to skills development at any level in degree programmes. Staff favoured an integrated approach to skill development and tutorial programmes seemed the best vehicle for delivery. The first stage in the innovation was a pilot project, premodularization.

The pilot project

To initiate core skills development a pilot project was carried out with a group of 80 students studying second-level biochemistry courses.

The aims

The aims of the project, derived from the context outlined in the introduction, can be summarized as:

- to introduce personal and professional skills development into bio-chemistry modules;
- to provide a consistent student experience in biochemistry tutorials;
- to give some coherence to flexible modular programmes;
- to improve student motivation.

There is a belief in the department that core skills are most effectively developed in a system which integrates them into the subject, explicitly identifying them, showing how they can be developed, while placing the responsibility for their development clearly with the student, and giving them assessment value.

The tutorial programme

A tutorial programme was compiled for use by the group of second-year students, which incorporated a structured scheme of instruction in core skills using a biochemical knowledge base. Each one-hour session had its specific aims in terms of biochemical knowledge and understanding and relevant core skills; thus the expected outcomes for the student were specified. Individual abilities at the start of the programme were identified by means of retained personal questionnaires; in this way students set personal targets for development. Awareness was raised of their own strengths and weaknesses in attitudes to work and core skills, including:

- learning processes;
- calculations, data handling and presentation;
- written communication skills;
- oral presentation skills;
- problem-solving strategies;
- exam preparation and technique;
- time management.

During the delivery of the programme specific tasks were set which challenged students, giving them opportunities for development of different aspects of their core skills. Tutors were given clear and detailed instructions for tutorials, ie aims, specific tasks to set, information resources from lectures, guidelines for skills development, specific feedback sheets for use and assessment grading criteria. An indication of activities can be obtained from Figure 5.1, which is an extract from a 'tutors guide'. It gives an outline of the structure of one term's programme, showing the tasks set to enable practice of core skills within specific knowledge areas. Tutorials were at two-weekly intervals.

Students were expected to present the outcomes of exercises such as those in Figure 5.1 to their peers, tutors or both during tutorial sessions. Important supportive aspects of the programme were:

- provision of detailed guidelines on how to acquire the various skills, in which the specific issues involved were raised;
- provision in tutorials of opportunities to practise skills using relevant material from the lecture course as a knowledge base;

TERM 1.	TASK	STUDY SKILL	KNOWLEDGE BASE	TUTORIAL FORMAT	MATERIALS
Tutorial 1	None assigned.			Introduction. Negotiate with students learning objectives of course and identify individual starting points. Establish the nature of this learning environment.	Study skill assessment questionnaires. Lecture course list. Learning outcomes information sheet.
Tutorial 2	Students to attend with written solutions to set calculations.	Biochemical calculations	Spectrophotometry and radioscopic methods.	Go through set calculations if students found them difficult. If they do go through two additional examples supplied. Spend last 15 mins devising a strategy for answering calculations. Write up as study skills notes if students want to.	Former exam questions, of calculations covering topics in column one supplied.
Tutorial 3	Students to attend with completed essays.	Essay writing.	Virus structure. Virus classification. Electron microscopy.	Students exchange essays and "mark" each others using feed-back sheets. Have time to read their own feed-back sheets and have a plenary session. Each one asked to state a positive outcome for themselves.	Four former exam questions covering topics in column 2. Essay performance feed-back sheets.
Tutorial 4	Three identified, briefed and prepared students to give 10 min oral presentations with set titles.	Oral presentations.	Bacterial cell synthesis of: 1.Envelope 2.Nucleic Acids 3.Protein synthesis	Three students to do 10 min oral presentations on set topics. Remaining students either i) take notes; ii) listen; followed by 5 min questions, then 4 min feed-back exchange. 5 min at end for presenters to identify the outcomes for themselves.	Three talk titles (column 2). OHP & materials. Oral presentation performance feed-back sheets.

Figure 5.1 *An extract from a tutor's guide*

- provision of written feedback from tutors and peers via completed forms;
- provision of structured opportunities for self-reflection from which learning outcomes are monitored.

An example of the practice process for one aspect of written communication skills is shown in Figure 5.2. A task was set and resources supplied and/or indicated. There was a tangible outcome which was used in formative assessment to support skills development. This was taking place in the informal atmosphere of the small group tutorial. The maximum number of students was ten, and tutors established an essential mutual support atmosphere from the beginning. Confidence could be gained and failure converted to success with help and positive guidance. The transferability of the skills within and outside degree programmes was stressed.

The outcomes

The pilot project has been carried out during the academic year 1992/3. Staff taking part in this project have found that having a structured and adequately resourced tutorial system has proved effective in that less time

Skill	Written communication: essay writing
Task	Essay titles
Resources	Essay writing guidelines. List of skills involved. Other knowledge base materials, eg library.
Evidence of outcomes	The finished essay. A list of skills used. Student's self-assessment and targets for development.
Formative assessment and support	At the tutorial students exchange essays. Using specific essay feedback sheets, students assess each other's work. Tutor collects marked essays and later makes own assessment. At the beginning of the next tutorial a few minutes is spent discussing the completed assessment sheets and on debriefing. It is pointed out that this skill will be practised again later in the year.

Figure 5.2 *Example of process for practising essay writing skills*

has been spent by them in preparing individual tutorials and that the preparation by the project organizers has led to consistent and improved quality in tutorials during busy teaching terms (this investment will be useful for several years). They have also found that peer group assessment of work has reduced their marking time. These outcomes point to maintenance and improvement of quality in a cost-effective way. Tutors observed an improvement in motivation which they perceived as stemming from clear student ownership of their own skills development programme, and an understanding of the relationship between core skills and final degree classification. Some staff confessed to a lack of confidence initially in teaching situations which did not have knowledge-based understanding as the sole focus, and indeed that is still the case among staff who have not yet been involved. Other staff found the structured arrangement too constricting, both to their own and student creativity. Some tutors were uncomfortable teaching out of their own field of expertise.

Staff who had not taken part in the project saw a need for staff development if personal transferable skill teaching were to be undertaken by all our staff. There was also some concern that knowledge content would be reduced if time were given to skill development and I have found this to be true.

Student responses were sought informally and with course evaluation questionnaires. Students welcome the explicit nature of the tutorial programme, gaining confidence from 'knowing what is expected of them', and an awareness of their own personal skills and their levels of competence in these. They appreciate additional opportunities to explore different methods of data presentation with time to reflect with peers and tutors on their effectiveness. Students began to understand terms like 'student-centred learning' and 'learning outcomes' and saw their relevance. The most notable outcome of the project for students is that their awareness is raised about their own personal and professional transferable skills and their levels of competence in specific areas. They became able to articulate this confidently, from the security of peer and tutor assessment, and tutorials were lively with students challenging tutor presentations and establishing their own focus to discussion.

The pilot tutorial programme has been a success. We now have a mechanism in place to:

- specifically identify the skills with which biochemistry graduates should be equipped;
- establish a method by which the personal development of these skills can be supported and integrated into undergraduate teaching;
- place responsibility for skills development clearly with the student;
- give academic value to skills.

The future

The strategy of the pilot project has been taken up, in the same form, in a structured first-level tutorial programme, having one student manual spanning several biochemistry modules, for single and combined honours undergraduates. As this programme is delivered through the academic year 1993/4 the response of students in Level I of their degree programme is somewhat different from those in their second level, who took part in the pilot project. It is apparent that Level I students require a 'gentler' approach, needing some passive learning situations as confidence-builders, and showing less enthusiasm for taking responsibility for their own skills development. These tutorials are not as lively as those in the pilot project.

During the first year of modular Level II delivery, academic staff with responsibility for modular curriculum development have designed tutorials with core skills practice in mind. When this academic year is complete we will take an overview of the potential for core skills development in Level II academic tutorials. In future a student-centred approach is planned for Level II students, based on their positive response to the pilot project. These students will be given a checklist of core skills. They will then be responsible, with advice from personal tutors, for their own action planning to develop these skills during their Level II study in biochemical and other modules. They will note down evidence of practice and competence against each skill. Reflection and review of progress will form the basis of Level II personal tutorial meetings, eg if a student has practised a specific data analysis skill in a laboratory sessions he or she could show evidence of practice (the laboratory report) and competence (the assessment grade and comments) to the personal tutor. In this way the implicit academic value of the skills is stressed.

Our medium term aims are: to extend our skills list to include practical skills and devise a system which will raise undergraduate awareness and competence in this area; and to extend the work we have begun on group work, peer support and formal skill assessment.

Conclusion

A strategy for the development of core skills, using tutorial programmes through modular degree structures, has been set up. It provides a strong foundation of personal and professional skills which apply in industry, academia and personal and social development. In the first year a structured introductory programme of skills development, with formative assessment and an integration of active and passive learning, is followed. Level II undergraduates have reached a maturity which facilitates a more active and student-centred approach. A programme will be negotiated by students, within guidelines, with a combination of self-, peer and tutor assessment generating some formal graded assessment.

The programmes seek to develop personal and professional transferable skills in students, and at the same time enhance their knowledge base by encouraging them to use it actively. The negotiated approach gives students ownership of their learning and promotes coherence in their individual modular honours degree programmes. Skills development is recorded and will be encouraged by the award of credit. Students and staff are challenged and stimulated by the use of new processes of learning and assessment. Students are made aware of their capabilities and staff extend their teaching expertise.

The knowledge base and the skills in our tutorial programmes may be altered but the same basic format can be used in any discipline to develop any personal transferable skill.

I wish to acknowledge the work of Dr Isobel Halliburton, Mrs Mary Cotterrell and Dr Paul Millner in the pilot project and Dr John Walker and Mrs Mary Cotterrell in the compilation of the Level I tutorial manual.

Chapter 6

Integrating Transferable Skills into Geography Through a Compulsory Core

Judy Chance

Introduction

The modular course structure at Oxford Brookes University has been designed to combine freedom of choice with coherent course structures within each field of study. In essence this involves two categories of module: compulsory core modules, which must be taken in a set order throughout the three or four years of the degree programme, and optional specialist modules, from which students make their own choices in order to fulfil the number of module credits required.

This structure allows students to take basic (or Stage 1) optional modules in their first, second or third year, while optional advanced (or Stage 2) modules may be taken in either their second or third year. While this has obvious advantages in enhancing flexibility it creates problems if one seeks to deliver a coherent skills development programme through these modules. While there are some instances in fields other than geography where successful completion of one optional module is a prerequisite for admission on to another one, we have sought to avoid this approach since it undermines the central benefit of any modular system: freedom of choice. The problem to be addressed is how this can be combined with the creation of coherent development of skills throughout the three years of study.

Geography at Oxford Brookes University is a single-field subject: this means, in effect, that it comprises half of a degree programme, and must be taken in association with another field (subject). The diverse nature of the subject and the range of other fields available to students mean that our students have a very varied set of combinations. In addition, it is also possible for selected modules from other fields to be counted as acceptable as geography module credits. This means that the only way in which we can ensure that particular ideas and skills are encountered by all students is to incorporate them into the core modules. Within the geography field there are six core modules plus the dissertation module:

Year 1	Term 1	Geography, environment and society
	Term 2	Britain's environment and society
	Term 3	Geographical inquiry
Year 2	Term 1	
	Terms 2 and 3	Geography of the contemporary world
Year 3	Term 1	Environmental pollution
	Term 2	
	Term 3	Environmental philosophy

As is clear from the above timetable, we have half of our core modules in the first year. This allows us to focus on skills development, with a steady progression through that year. For such a coherent programme it is however essential to plan the incorporation of both skills and ideas very carefully, a process which requires very considerable investment in course design.

Four years ago we initiated a new set of core modules in the planning of which, having established the academic framework, skills development was given a high profile, building on pioneering work within the unit (Gold *et al.*, 1991; Keene, 1988). Clearly the first stage had to be the identification of the relevant skills, a task of considerable complexity. Not only did we need to identify broad categories such as communication and information technology, but we also had to consider the various levels of complexity and the subdivisions within these classes. The second stage, integration of skills into the academic structure, was rather more straightforward, although ensuring progression rather than repetition requires careful consideration of the tasks involved and of the criteria used for assessment. Having decided at which points various skills were to be introduced and expanded, we then had to consider how to deliver appropriate training and, finally, how to assess the skills achievements of students and, in particular, how to balance this with assessment of their academic achievement.

Identification of core skills

In broad terms we identified six main groupings of skills, but the identification and allocation of skill categories is far from being a hard and fast process. In the early stages of our planning of the new core programme we decided to focus on a pair of skills in each of the three first year modules:

Term 1	Writing and literary analysis
	Groupwork and collaborative skills
Term 2	Speaking and debating
	Word-processing
Term 3	Numeracy and data handling
	Field techniques and research planning

While these are the main focal points of each module, skills already covered are developed further in subsequent modules. In the advanced compulsory modules these six categories are expanded to include more advanced skills, including in particular the development of critical thinking and evaluation skills. At this stage it becomes clear that the distinction between transferable skills and traditional academic skills is rather an artificial one.

Integration of skills into the core modules

In each case, the starting point for planning a module has to be its academic role: the series of core modules is designed to introduce the central theme of the relationship between society and environment and to build up an increasingly informed, complex and questioning approach to that relationship. The optional specialist modules allow students to focus in on certain detailed aspects, while preserving the same underlying theme.

The diversity of the material and the techniques used by geographers gives us an unusually wide range of opportunities for skills development in which the skills are integral to the academic discipline. For example, numeracy skills are just as important as literacy skills; the ability to use simple surveying instruments is as essential as the ability to chair a discussion. This is what makes it relatively easy to work out a programme in which skills development runs in parallel with academic development, rather than having a separate skills module. Because of the small number of academic staff in the geography unit (only 6.8) in some cases we have chosen to buy in expertise from other sources. For instance, in cooperation with the university's computer services unit, we have produced a dedicated workbook for self-paced learning of SPSS within the first of the two fieldwork based modules, geographical inquiry. The major area of weakness in our skills development programme is the lack of any foreign language component within the field.

Our first-year programme includes an introduction to the full range of skills identified, but it is fair to say that particular emphasis is placed upon certain skills, chief among which are the following four areas (but listed in no particular order of precedence). The first is the area of groupwork skills. This has for some time been an arena in which the geography unit has done major pioneering work (Jenkins and Pepper, 1988), and its development is carried right through the programme, introducing students to a wide range of different group situations. The early development of the requisite skills stands students in good stead through the rest of their course and, we hope, the rest of their lives.

A second area of emphasis is that of information technology, including not only computing but also the ability to employ effective library search techniques and to identify relevant sources of information in, for example, local government. The inclusion of two fieldwork-based modules (plus the option of the dissertation module) offers a good deal of scope for primary data collection and analysis, not to mention hands-on experience of word-processing, both for documents and for larger-scale poster presentations.

A third area of emphasis is communication skills. Right from the start students are required to employ a range of presentations: group or individual; handwritten, word-processed, graphic or oral; formal or informal; self-assessed, peer-assessed, staff-assessed or unassessed. Once again, this issue of peer assessment and self-assessment is one in which the geography unit has been a pioneer. While it requires careful clarification of all the assessment criteria, there is no doubt that it encourages reflective self-evaluation and enhances subsequent performance. This is perhaps especially important in some aspects of skills development, such as groupwork and oral presentation, in which self-awareness is an essential element.

A fourth area of emphasis is the development of critical and analytical thinking. While this begins in the first term, inevitably it really flowers in the later stages of the programme when students have had time to develop a greater grasp of their discipline. Thus it is in their second and, particularly, their third year that they are required to move beyond a synthetic study of the literature to promulgate and support their own arguments, to be able to identify particular approaches and also to be able, when required, to present material from a viewpoint other than their own.

As students move through their second year the only core module is based around a week-long field-course in the west of Ireland. While this draws on a number of those skills developed in the first year, it introduces a new dimension: the collection of information and the establishment of a research programme from a distance. In particular, the moribund art of letter-writing becomes central, since small groups of students are required to arrange their own investigations in Ireland, setting up any interviews and visits in advance, so that their time in Ireland is used to best effect. This module also introduces a new form of presentation: the use of an informal journal for each person to keep a record of their subjective perceptions and experiences.

In their final year, students complete the two remaining core subject modules. While both of these seek further to hone groupwork and presentation skills, the first one involves a carefully structured peer assessment element, in which peer assessment accounts for one- third of the final mark for a major group presentation. This substantial allocation of marks is supported by a detailed set of criteria (see the Appendix at the end of this chapter). The final module's special contribution is in its requirement that students learn to recognize and to employ a range of value systems. This is seen as the final stage in their development as critical and analytical thinkers, a development which effectively involves both skills-based and academic growth.

Delivery of skills training

The geography unit's policy is to concentrate staff support for students into the first year, with teaching done in small groups of no more than 12–14 students. This has been achieved through the use of work-books written by the whole staff team to replace lectures. Each of the core modules is team taught, with each lecturer teaching on two out of the three. In addition to the small seminar groups, in which some elements of skills training are embedded, there are a number of workshop sessions which focus specifically on one skill. These cover groupwork skills, formal writing skills, the use of word-processing and statistical packages and certain data collection techniques. There is also a simulation exercise, an early step on the way to recognizing and applying alternative value systems.

The goal of this intensive investment of staff resources into the first year is to help students progress towards independent learning as soon as possible. In the remaining core modules students increasingly take on responsibility for their own and their peers' learning, with staff being seen as one of a range of resources available for students' use. For example, in the second fieldwork-based module, geography and the contemporary world, lecturers act as supervisors of what are, in effect, independent group projects. As and when requested by students, workshops can be arranged on specific techniques, advice can be sought on suitable research designs and students can also be directed to particular specialist training sessions provided elsewhere in the university.

Our early experience of the new core programme has led to some changes. While it is relatively simple to arrange for skills training in such concrete areas as computing and statistics, there are other less straightforward areas. Typically these centre around issues concerning social behaviour and the most troublesome one has consistently been groupwork. This year we have introduced specific training sessions on groupwork, which are run in the first term of the first year. A combination of activities was employed to explore three main areas: what makes a group a group rather than a bunch of individuals? What roles are required within a group? What are the most worrying problems and how can they be tackled? This initial session is built upon in later sessions that term and in subsequent terms.

Assessment of skills

The policy within the geography unit is that, for any assessment exercise, the criteria must be explicitly laid out in the course guidelines, so that students know exactly what is required. For different tasks the balance between skills and academic content will vary, but clearly any task is likely to include both elements. The peer assessment guidelines from the environmental pollution module (see the Appendix) are a useful indicator of the criteria used and of the clarity required.

Conclusion

Within the degree of flexibility encouraged by the modular course structure the only way to ensure a coherent programme of skills development which is not divorced from the academic content is to build it into a series of compulsory core modules which stretch across the full length of the course.

This allows the skills to develop in tandem with the intellectual content, so that, as more sophisticated techniques are required for more demanding work, they are made available. What we label as 'personal transferable skills' are, of course, tools of our academic trade: simply because they are also seen as particularly useful in the wider world is no good reason to seek to seclude them into a separate ghetto. Indeed, to follow this strategy runs the very real risk of labelling them as, at best, peripheral to the degree course and thus reducing their beneficial impact on student performance.

References

Gold, J et al. (1991) *Teaching Geography in Higher Education: A manual of good practice*, Oxford: Basil Blackwell.

Jenkins, A and Pepper, D (1988) *Enhancing Empolyability and Educational Experience: A manual on teaching communication and groupwork skills in higher education, Standing Conference on Educational Development*, Occasional Paper No 27, Oxford Polytechnic.

Keene, P (1988) 'Teaching physical geographers to talk', *Journal of Geography in Higher Education*, 12, 85–95.

Appendix: Advice on allocating marks for conference presentations

Criteria	A = 70% or above	Bc = 60-69%	B = 50-59%	C = 40-49%	F = 39% or below
	First class, a rare grade.	Upper second class, a very good grade.	Lower second class, a good grade (competent, but some limitations).	Third class, a poor/weak grade.	Failed, not yet competent.
Communication	All speakers are clear, articulate and interesting.	Retains interest throughout but not as stimulating as an A-grade.	Variable quality, eg one or two speakers too fast, not always clear or reading from notes.	Many speakers give rushed presentations or read from notes. Does not always make sense. Starts and ends weakly/poorly.	Too many speakers unclear or reading from notes. Does not make sense.
Content (Relevance and knowledge)	Contains an argument, which is consistently very well argued, backed up with very good evidence and examples. Keeps to relevant issues throughout. Excellent understanding conveyed by whole group, and familiarity with the topic.	Not as consistently well-argued or as critical and relevant as an A-grade, but there are recognizable arguments and themes, and more than just one or two members know the topic well.	Too much description. Variable depth of knowledge shown by group. Perhaps lacking in examples and/or justification of points expressed. Needs to be more critical.	Generally unconvincing or too simplistic in the arguments offered. Not much evidence for arguments except at general level. Lacking in critical thought, over-descriptive.	Too many erroneous or unsubstantiated general points/arguments offered. Lack of evidence of understanding of issues or of having undertaken the necessary reading.
Organization	Clearly stated aims, excellent flow and structure. Excellent group cooperation. Arguments and themes follow each other in a logical way.	Clearly stated aims, but flow/structure and group cooperation not as good as an A-grade. May spend too much time on one stage of the argument.	Aims need some clarification or flow, structure and group cooperation need improvement. Exceeds time limit (indicating lack of rehearsal).	Aims unclear. Group not functioning together very well. Exceeds time limit or uses only half the time available (indicating failure to rehearse).	Aims unclear or not stated. Group cooperation minimal. Flow and structure of presentation not evident.
Answers to questions, audience involvement	Whole group answers questions clearly, effectively and knowledgeable. Attempt to involve audience in other ways.	Not all the group able to answer questions clearly, effectively and knowledgeably. Some answers need improvement.	Some limitations in knowledge/ understanding evident in several answers. Most of the audience uninvolved and uninterested.	Answers weak or largely waffle from most of the group.	Too many poor or incorrect answers. Some questions not answered.

Chapter 7

A Very 'English' Profile? A Model for Subject-based Development, and an Argument for Peculiar Practices in Profiling

Rob Pope

Opening questions and context

How far should the development of supposedly 'core' or 'transferable' skills be divorced from subject-based knowledges and practices? How can students be genuinely empowered - yet also guided – through the learning process? More particularly, what part can course journals and student profiling play in all these processes and how are such learning strategies to relate to formal assessment and certification? These are the questions this chapter addresses. To do so it draws on the experience of designing and running courses developing subject-based skills and student profiling in an English studies field within a modular scheme. Some 400 English studies students are engaged in this process annually, and all of them take English with one of some 40 other subjects (ranging from computing to biology, and with publishing, history, education and modern languages as the most common combinations).

But there is a more immediate institutional context and prompt for this chapter. This is the current, highly contentious debate on how precisely skills development is to be coordinated throughout my own and other institutions in higher education: how far we are to go for centralized and/or course-based models; and how far 'profiling' is to be student-centred and/or staff-monitored. It will be clear from the following pages where I (along with many immediate colleagues and students) see ourselves standing in this debate. However, it is hoped that the following account will be of assistance to others grappling with similar problems and possibilities, not only in humanities subjects nor even only in modular courses. Here, then, is an overview of the kinds of skills and knowledges our English studies students are currently required to practise and how their development is monitored. For convenience and clarity, we distinguish four aspects of the process:

- overall subject-area aims
- module descriptions
- guidance on course journals
- suggested formats for subject-based summary profiles.

Overall subject-area aims

In the *English Studies Field Handbook*, held by all students and staff, the general aims of the subject are expressed in terms of the following broad 'learning outcomes':

By the end of the English Studies part of your programme, you should be able to:

(1) communicate effectively in speech and writing, individually and in groups, drawing on an appropriate and effective range of presentational materials and skills;

(2) analyse many kinds of text in English with a high degree of technical precision combined with an awareness of the critical, linguistic, creative, theoretical and historical issues and processes involved;

(3) be able to demonstrate an understanding of fundamental issues and processes in the study of at least two historical periods;

(4) choose a mode of critical exposition which is appropriate to a particular text, chosen with a particular audience or readership in mind, and likely to be effective for your particular purposes;

(5) decide how best to apply those skill and knowledges you have acquired and developed to activities subsequent to your degree, whether in employment, post-graduate study or leisure.

These overall subject-based aims are not, of course, offered as models for everyone to follow. Subject areas vary hugely in orientations, methods and materials. Moreover, even for English studies such aims are far from comprehensive or complete, and they would doubtless prove contentious in some other institutions. None the less, these 'overall aims' are offered as an example of the *kind* of thing which, it is suggested, every subject area in a modular course should produce – and perhaps in any course. Moreover, this should be produced *by* members of that subject area (staff and students) primarily *for* themselves. What is required is an initial act of *self*-definition, *self*-determination and *self*-presentation.

Notwithstanding, such 'aims' may then be collected and coordinated for the institution as a whole. It should be particularly stressed, however, that the aim of the latter exercise is *not* the reductive 'boiling down' of all these various subject aims into some grotesquely homogenized list of supposedly 'core skills'. For such lists tend not only to be highly arbitrary and deeply contentious, they also turn out to be intellectually facile and practically useless. No. The whole point of a *consolidated* list is that it is just that:

consolidated but not concentrated; coordinated but not reduced; unifiable but not uniform. It actually encourages -and does not just allow, let alone prohibit – practices which bristle with specificities, even while underscoring some common – and in the event rather obvious – denominators (communicative skills, capacity to work in groups, etc). In this way, the cardinal strengths of modular courses (flexibility and student choice) can be maintained. Yet there is no pretence at a bogus totality or, still worse, a kind of 8-, 10- or 12-ingredient recipe for 'what makes a graduate from institution X worth buying'. In place of a blandly monolithic mission statement and mere flashy advertising there could also be an authentically plural voice expressing divergent as well as common interests.

Module descriptions

In the descriptions of specific modules we emphatically prefer that the definition, development and assessment of skills be integrated into existing sections. That is, we do not think it proper or valuable to include a separate section specifically labelled 'skills' ('core', 'transferable', 'subject-specific' or otherwise). For one thing, distinctions between 'core' ('transferable'?) and 'subject-specific' ('non-transferable'?) prove deeply divisive and contentious. They also inevitably increase the bureaucratic freight (and sheer length) of module descriptions without actually improving their effectiveness and clarity. Instead, we favour some such integration as that illustrated in the following module description. This one describes a first-year, first-term module called 'Language, literature, discourse I'. I shall quote it at length, though not in full, for it is the sheer specificity and detail – not simply the general principles – of such descriptions which is important.

Course description. An introduction to the terms and techniques of linguistic analysis, with systematic practice in textual transformation and intervention.

Educational aims. These may be expressed in terms of the skills and knowledges the course is designed to develop. By the end of the course students should have developed four things:

(1) a good basic sense of how the language – particularly the English language – is structured and how it is used;
(2) a practical understanding of the chief relevant models of communication, discourse and sign-theory;
(3) a handy kit of terms and techniques to describe varieties of English in use – in speech and writing, in live conversation and the printed and electronic media, in 'literary' and 'non-literary' texts;
(4) the confidence to challenge and change any stretch of language, and so show up its distinctive strategies and structures.

The overall aim may be summed up as the improvement of students' analytical and expressive capacities, and an enhanced awareness of language as a source of power and of pleasure... .

Set texts. ...The function of the anthology [a recent anthology of British-Caribbean poetry] is to provide an introduction to a variety of Englishes and a variety of poetic forms and performance modes in cultural frames which for many students should prove new and challenging. The result should be both a dislocation of established patterns of reading/listening and an encouragement to engage with fresh patterns of writing and performance. ...

Learning and teaching. This will take place through two large group sessions ('lectures') and one small group session weekly. All of the sessions. large and small, include bouts of practical work, presentations (by both students and staff) and exercises.

Assessment

Coursework: textual analysis to be presented orally in tutorial and last not more than 10 minutes, plus discussion. ...Brief supporting notes (300 words max) consisting chiefly of headings and written 'cues' for the presentation will be handed in immediately afterwards. A more detailed brief and set of assessment criteria are supplied.

2-hour exam (75%): written textual analysis based on a short extract accompanied by specific exercises.

Crucially, the above module is not designed in isolation. It is part of an overall subject strategy relating most immediately to a subsequent English studies first-year double module, 'Texts problems and approaches' (for which the former is 'recommended' but not 'pre-requisite'). In the case of the follow-up module, for instance, there is more emphasis on collective agenda-setting and presentation (including one wholly student-led session per week with no member of staff present). There is also a different (50/50) balance of coursework and exam: the former divided equally between creative-interventive work and traditional essay; the latter reinforcing this procedure in a two-hour exam.

Similar, systematically varied agendas *integrating* the development and assessment of skills with knowledges are currently being made explicit for all other English field modules (in some cases these were there implicitly and in practice some time ago). The improved results and the generally enthusiastic course evaluations confirm that students are more fully engaged than previously, both with the acquisition of knowledges *and* the development of skills. Indeed, the knowledges/skills distinction itself frequently dissolves in students' own monitoring of their progress as educational subjects/agents (ie, learners) even as they explore the development of their academic discipline as an a configuration of educational subject (ie, bodies of knowledge – 'know how' plus 'know what'). This brings us to the next, perhaps most crucial aspects of the process.

Course journals and summary profiles: private processes and public products

As signalled by the question mark in the title of this chapter, there can in fact be no prizes for a unique and peculiarly 'English' profile. The practice of using course journals (logs or diaries, etc) is both widespread and well developed and the related practice of summative 'profiling' may become so. However, what follows may at least serve to underscore the value of such reflective and critical commentaries in an area of higher education – and perhaps many areas -where their use is as yet marginal or completely neglected.

Course journals, for us, have come to be the heart of the student's process of self-monitoring and reflective learning. In English, we are concentrating these at two strategic points: towards the close of Stage I (in a module spanning Terms 2 and 3); and at the close of Stage II (in the synoptic module in Terms 2 and 3 of the final year). The *English Studies Field Handbook* and specific course materials offer detailed guidelines for the keeping of the course journals. Every week the student is required to focus on the three primary moments of the learning process (preparation, participation and retrospect); and from one week to the next he or she is encouraged to observe a recursive as well as a cumulative pattern of learning (reflecting upon overall progress and orientation). The criteria proposed are therefore both general (I quote): 'speaking; listening; working on your own; working with others; planning; etc' and specific: 'making detailed summaries of reading and research, analytical techniques and theoretical models used'.

A crucial aspect of the course journal is its *privacy*. This is, again in the words of the English Studies Handbook, 'your own document, for your own private use (though you may wish to share notes with colleagues)'. Such confidentiality follows from the primary purpose of the course journal, which is 'to develop the habit of conscious self-evaluation, with the associated process of setting individual action plans'. This purpose, we are convinced, cannot be fulfilled if students feel they are going to be observed, judged and formally assessed on every single thing they record each week. 'Going public' and being assessed are thus the final but not overriding stages of the process.

Each student is required to submit a *summary (subject-based) profile* at the close of Stages I and II (ie, the ends of first and final years). These summary profiles are to be based on the course journals, a maximum of 500 words each and must be submitted for the student to be deemed to have completed the courses to which they are specifically attached (modules 2306, 2392). Consequently, these profiles are not assigned a separate mark in and for themselves, but they do form part of the overall course requirement. Again, guidelines on the kinds of criteria to be considered are supplied. I quote:

You should review:

- the kinds of KNOWLEDGE(S) you have developed (textual, critical, historical, theoretical, etc)
- the direct relevance and applicability – or otherwise – of these knowledges to (1) your immediate personal and social situation, your present needs and desires, and (2) your longer term life and career goals
- the kinds of SKILLS you have developed (personal and interpersonal, oral and written (including presentation), individual and collective; analytical and argumentational; research; word-processing, etc)
- the direct relevance and applicability of these skills (as above for 'knowledges'...).

Again, then, we seek to maintain a connection as well as a distinction between those perennially tricky concepts 'knowledge(s)' (note the plural) and 'skills'. At the same time we are keen to resist the current trend towards homogenization represented by the recent arrival, 'competences' (which many people bandy around but few define). Moreover, these guidelines are only broadly *de*scriptive; and certainly they are neither *pre*scriptive nor *pro*scriptive. For, in line with an overall philosophy of genuine *self*-evaluation and *personal* responsibility, we deliberately avoid any insistence on a fixed and uniform format (other than that the final texts be 500 words maximum). Students are therefore expressly advised that:

The precise formulation, articulation and mode of presentation of each summary profile is up to you...[because] the most immediate and important 'subject' engaged in the educational process is you. It is therefore your business to give the only profile of this course that ultimately matters: your own.

In other words, to use the currently f(l)avoured terminology, the 'learning outcomes' we are mainly interested in are the kinds of 'learning' students themselves judge they have 'come out' with. Moreover, as students are also reminded, such 'summary profiles' may readily be turned into CVs, though again the emphasis is on this being done under the student's own hand and not in the form of some institutionally-uniform 'skills' transcript supplied by a deadening combination of staff and computers.

Concluding propositions and questions

I shall summarize this chapter by sounding some openly contentious yet, I hope, constructive notes. They take the form of, first, some general propositions and then some specific questions. The propositions are manifestly manifesto-like and meant to generate heat as well as light. The questions invite you (the reader/learner/teacher) to transform that heat and light into possible answers with respect to your own educational subjects in your own institutional context (for by definition I can know little or nothing of these).

General propositions

To be successful, effective and genuinely empowering, course design:

- **must** fully integrate the definition, development and assessment of skills into subject-specific practice;
- **must not** nor be tacked on as a parallel or additional system
- **must** be flexible enough to encourage a genuine variety and plurality of student- and subject-centred skills and knowledges
- **must not** attempt to impose a standardized – and still less a uniform – list of requisite skills and knowledges for all students, regardless of their individual needs and interests and the distinctive natures of their subjects

- **must** encourage critical, reflexive and transformative education – as opposed to blandly 'transferable skills', and blindly instrumental knowledges
- **must not**, therefore, let the 'training' tail wag the 'educational' dog.

Specific questions

- Subject-area aims.
  Does your subject area have a declared set of overall aims? If so, what are they, and how far do they integrate skills with subject-specific knowledges? If not, have a go at sketching such overall aims.
- Individual module/course descriptions.
  Which of the following is practised in the formal description of modules/courses in your subject area (and perhaps in your institution as a whole)? Do you: (a) integrate skills and knowledges into descriptions of 'educational aims', 'learning patterns' and 'assessment', etc? (b) separate out skills and knowledges into distinct sections (perhaps with further subdivisions into 'core', 'transferable' and 'subject-specific', etc)? (c) do something else?
- Course journals, work diaries, etc.
  Does your subject area encourage or require the use of these: how, where, when and why? If not, what other kinds of continuous, reflective and self-monitoring process do you use (eg, periodic forums, periodic student-student and/or student-staff interviews, etc.)? How far are these processes 'private' or 'public', and how far do they lead to specific products which are assessed? (By whom?)
- Summary (subject-based) profiles.
  Does your subject area require each student to submit a summary retrospect of where he or she has been going in that subject, and a provisional prospect of where he or she may subsequently be taking it (both within education and beyond)? If so, what form does this take and is it assessed? If not, why not? If otherwise, how and why?

SECTION C:
DEVELOPING SKILLS THROUGH STUDENT CHOICE AND INDEPENDENT STUDY

Chapter 8

Generic Skills for Science Undergraduates: How Modularity Made it Possible

Mike Williams and Richard Horobin

We have for many years been university teachers of laboratory science, theoretical and practical. Much of that effort was directed towards student acquisition of specific knowledge bases and specific laboratory skills. This was done in the expectation that our graduates would largely find placements or employment in subject-related situations. We work in the University of Sheffield, which is a civic university, of about 12,000 students. This institution was founded as a college over a hundred years ago, and has a distinguished history in scientific research. Much of the science teaching devolves around laboratory work. Lately a modular teaching structure has been introduced throughout the faculty of pure science.

Nearly a decade ago our institution produced a discussion document concerning the teaching of personal transferable skills. This received widespread formal approval in public; and widespread criticism, even jeering, over the coffee cups. Nevertheless, we responded to this document by floating a departmental scheme for training of this type, for a small third-year science class. The outcome was that we developed, and for several years ran, a set of four afternoon classes with the overt theme of 'What will you do after you graduate?'. This provided opportunities for students to speak in public and to think on their feet. A variety of modalities were used: talking in equal-time pairs to one other person; addressing the whole class; and interviewing and being interviewed.

To these classes our colleagues remained at best indifferent, and at worst rather aggressive. On one occasion, during a departmental staff meeting, we were accused of 'putting at risk the psychological health of the students'. Once the classes were set up, and despite our persistent efforts, we never succeeded in recruiting a single colleague to participate in a single class and, mysteriously and without apparent calculation, the classes were – year on year – omitted from the department's formal teaching timetable.

More consequential were the students' attitudes. These students were, at the time classes were run, very concerned with final-year research projects. Going to a formal class - especially perhaps an oddball class, sometimes thought dubious by their supervisors – was not a priority. We persisted, and would go around the laboratories on the mornings of the classes, whipping-in participants. Even though nominally compulsory, not everyone attended. At the end of the set of classes, students who did attend considered that they had learned a great deal. Feedback sheets were predominantly positive.

However, after four years we were beaten down. We stopped running the classes. And we never did get them on to the timetable. But times change. A year ago, with our science degree courses having been 'modularized', the department was seeking new modules. So again we found ourselves offering to run classes in the personal skills arena. This time we offered, designed, set up and ran a 12-afternoon module entitled 'Communications and presentation skills'. In our first attempt at this, 26 students signed up and took part.

There was a theme running through this, namely to have the students repeatedly face the question, 'What am I going to be doing next year?'. Hence many practical tasks and exercises dealt with finding information about jobs, writing letters to prospective employers, writing CVs and so on. This allowed us, while retaining face validity, to encourage students to stretch their horizons, for instance, asking 'What do I hope I'll be doing in ten years time?', and dealing with a variety of simulations of professional situations. A variety of modes of communication were explored: spoken, written and graphical, involving telephones, fax machines and electronic mail.

Some idea of the content of the module can be gained from the Appendix to this chapter. The style of classes emphasized personal responsibility in a safe environment. Sessions were highly participative and highly structured, even though student feedback described them as 'informal' and 'relaxed'. This was achieved by two experienced teachers working flexibly as an ad-libbing double act within a pre-planned frame.

There are several differences, and one striking similarity, between this module and our earlier efforts. This time the module was a formal element in the students' timetable, no problems there. The module was four times the contact hours of the earlier classes. We also met on a twice-a-week basis, which was three times more often. This time we covered a wider range of activities, from IT in computer rooms to tasks in the shops of the city centre.

We did however still experience difficulty in recruiting other teachers, the two exceptions being a returning expatriate with an MBA from an American university, and on several occasions a teacher from continuing adult education. In addition, several members of the technical staff became enthusiastic confederates.

This time, what were the outcomes? The attendance was exceptional. Moreover, most students saw the module as being useful, not oddball, even when aspects of it angered them. What angered them? Assessment. A large proportion of the students were explicitly positive concerning their experience of the module, many saying things such as, 'The atmosphere enabled me to overcome my nerves' and 'Informative, enjoyable and very useful'. But was this just a 'feel-good effect', or did the module make differences in the rest of the students' academic life? One indication of useful outcomes concerns an assessed essay subsequently written by a subset of the students on the module. Unlike previous years, students came to discuss the essay with their tutor, and phoned up a variety of people in other institutions, for instance The Imperial Cancer Research Fund, seeking information.

Are today's students different? Have we become better teachers? Or is modularization magic? Perhaps all three factors are relevant. It is true that today's undergraduates are different to those of a decade ago. They look out from the institution in different directions. Few science students any longer regard science as their vocation and yet they now regard personal skills as relevant to their needs and 'useful'. Their perceived needs seem to have changed.

And yes, of course we've got better at teaching. We've been on, and taught on, many training courses. Moreover we've done a lot more growing up in the past ten years.

What about 'modular magic'? It also seems an important part of our second-time-around success. It provided an immediate face validity with students. This time we were running 'a module just like any other'. It gave a copper-bottomed case for a budget. And once chosen by students, the knock-on effect included a greater acknowledgement from our peers. For the first time, the classes are on the timetable.

Appendix: Individual classes in the 'Communication and presentation skills' module

1. 'Where do I go from here?' The Interview. This class also provides an introduction to the content and approach of the module as a whole.
2. Looking for jobs/applying for training. Practical steps in choosing, finding and obtaining preliminary information.

3. Writing about yourself, from summarizing research progress to records of achievement and CVs.
4. Some mechanics of written self-presentation. Electronic aids: word-processors simple and less so, spelling and grammar checkers, desk-top publishing, and more.
5. Getting the most out of modern communication systems. Email on the campus network and beyond, fax agencies, express document services – even the telephone.
6. Presenting yourself in person: public speaking, scientifically and less so.
7. Finding information from electronic sources.
8. An opportunity for an informal review of progress: 'Will you just look at this?'.
9. Formalities of travel. Obtaining travel documents, buying tickets, planning timetables, costing accommodation.
10. Getting your message across graphically. Plus several chances to practice assessment: a self-assessment, assessment of your peers, and assessment of your teachers.
11. Using the telephone: presenting yourself in person? Practical exercises in information-gathering and persuasion.
12. 'But is it really ME?'. Think about personal values and their practical relevance to your choices.

Chapter 9

Differing Approaches to Independent Study

Kate Murray and Chris Gore

Introduction

One of the advantages of modularity is that it facilitates the development of independent study modules across an institution; this further increases student choice and flexibility of programme selection. In different institutions, however, the independent study can vary considerably in scope, form and method of organization. This chapter provides a comparison of independent study as it has been developed in two universities and identifies common aspects and academic issues which have been addressed in different ways. A comparison of different forms of independent study enables the benefits to be identified and can provide guidelines on the issues which need to be resolved by academics considering such innovations. Benefits include the development of a wide range of capabilities and an enhanced student experience. The two universities on which the studies have been based are Coventry University and the University of Derby. Coventry University has approximately 15,000 students and modularized all its undergraduate programmes in 1991. The University of Derby has grown in the last three years from 5,000 to 10,000 students. It introduced a modular scheme two years ago, on which one-fifth of students are enrolled.

What is independent study?

The concept of independent study can vary and is open to different interpretations. However, the two institutions being compared have a similar understanding of the concept. For example:

Independent study is student-initiated work carried out by the student for assessment as part of a course. Independent study is carried out in substitution for specified course units within a named degree course. (Coventry University)

The CAMS independent study programme should be regarded as a key element of your course; it provides a unique opportunity to develop your own particular personal interests and abilities in a fashion and at a pace which suits you. (University of Derby – Credit accumulation modular degree scheme)

In academic style, independent study can range from the traditional literature reviews, survey work and experiment-based projects to the more innovative projects, such as helping voluntary organizations or enhancing the life of the university. The setting for the work might be the university or outside it in the community. The product or output of independent study could be a report, a design, a computer programme, a work of art or advice to a client, as well as the more traditional dissertation. Examples of independent study include:

- painting a mural within or on the exterior of buildings for community use by schools or community centres;
- helping voluntary organizations to provide more effective and efficient services for their members, for example, a women's health group, equal opportunities policy and a housing cooperative;
- designing computer software for payroll systems or information on courses for young people;
- designing and producing a newspaper;
- making a feasibility study of setting-up a shop as a community business;
- undertaking environmental conservation work;
- undertaking field research investigating the employment opportunities for ethnic minorities;
- carrying out laboratory-based investigations of a scientific nature;
- preparing a traditional dissertation based on a literature research concerned with, for example, film and television, or women in 19th-century literature;
- carrying out market research investigating the possibilities of franchising for small businesses.

Academic issues

Differences between institutions in the approach to independent study emerge in relation to the resolution of a number of academic issues: the scope of the study, the criteria used, assessment, organization and supervision.

The scope of the study

One of the first issues we faced was that of deciding which areas/subjects were considered suitable for independent study. In both institutions, independent study could include dissertations, project work, either laboratory-based or field survey work and exhibitions. However, in one institution it could also include social and organizational activities such as community health schemes and 'enhancing the life of the university'. The main determinant of the suitability of the subject material in this case is that it must ensure that the course objectives are satisfied.

Given that independent study can be very wide in its scope, the extent of the breadth of study allowed must be decided. Will the work be fairly narrowly defined within the traditional project work, or will it allow a much wider approach to encourage a number of forms of activity which would not normally be included in traditional project work? This raises further questions concerned with ensuring academic rigour, the ability of academic staff to satisfactorily supervise or monitor student activities and the involvement of external referees.

Criteria

In one institution, a very strong emphasis is placed on the formation of criteria for assessment as unique to the project in hand and linked to the aims and objectives of the project. These criteria are formulated by the student at the proposal stage, usually with guidance from a tutor. They are then either approved or rejected by the course committee or its representatives. The other institution concentrates on negotiating criteria between supervisors and students, with the aim of encouraging a wide range of activities and outputs, yet within a strong academic frame of reference. The students benefit from guidance from supervisors but may, in some circumstances, feel constrained, depending on the flexibility of the people concerned.

In contrast, the traditional approach is for staff to set criteria for assessment and students to design their project or independent study to fit within the confines of these criteria. This approach has the advantage of being 'safe' and following a known and accepted path towards knowledge acquisition, but may not encourage such a creative approach, nor such a sense of 'ownership', and can lead to a narrower range of acceptable projects or areas of independent study.

Assessment

Another contentious issue which requires resolution, and for which there is no 'hard and fast' rule, is assessment. Given that there is a wide range of independent study, it is no surprise that there is a wide variety of assessment methods. The output from such a range of independent study varies from traditional written work to development of personal skills, interpersonal skills and organizational skills. So assessment may vary from a traditional dissertation to a shorter project, writing-up field or laboratory-based work, to an exhibition of artwork or designs.

In one institution, student performance is normally assessed on the product of the work, which might be a report, a design, a work of art or an achievement in community service. These latter can be assessed by a diary or logbook (personal or kept by others). However, because the outputs are necessarily intangible, verification of work is not a simple matter. In both institutions, the negotiation of the student setting of criteria can lead to multidimensional assessments. So written work, presentations and physical outputs have to be combined into one mark. This has the advantage of covering several aspects of the work undertaken but can lead to a heavy workload on both students and staff. Both institutions require the output to be amenable to external evaluation which, given the variety of forms it can take, can provide problems. It does have the advantage of encouraging the use of a wider range of externals in order to gain expertise not always found in traditional external examiners.

Organization

As would be expected, independent study plays a varying role in the course programme in the two institutions. In one institution, the modular scheme is not universal, but the independent study is 'an essential component of the honours degree stage', whereas in the other institution all undergraduates have the opportunity for independent study, but it is not an essential part of their programme and cannot replace core modules of any programme.

There is also a difference in the level. In one, it operates at Level 3 and in the other at Levels 2 or 3, depending on the independent study devised. In both institutions, it provides credits: in one, a single credit module of 15 and in the other, a double credit module of 30. A year's full-time study normally amounts to 120 credits.

Clearly, where an independent study module is a core element of a final year, it is more risky for a student to undertake to produce an innovative output using an unusual method than to follow a conventional route to produce a project or a dissertation. In deciding where to place independent study in a programme, consideration of such issues may lead to encouraging more experimental approaches by students if the module is not central to the degree.

Supervision

As with all forms of teaching innovation, the resource requirements are a major concern. As independent study relates to a specially tailored module, the servicing requirement could be expensive. Traditional project and dissertation supervision is resource-intensive, with tuition being provided on a one-to-one basis at regular supervisory meetings, adopting the research degrees model. It must be remembered, however, that this is not a traditional project. If the object of independent study is to develop those skills associated with a high level of student-centred learning and control, it can be argued that there should be little staff involvement.

While neither institution adopts the research model in its strictest sense, there are different approaches to supervision. In the institution where independent study is a core element, the recommended staff allowance is between 10 and 20 hours per student. Some subjects conduct interviews with students on a group basis in workshops, while others use individual interviews. The nature of the work and the interests of the students dictate the model adopted. In the other institution, where the module is optional and the undergraduate programme often includes a research-type project, the independent study module is not closely supervised, except in exceptional circumstances. Emphasis is instead placed on a detailed specification of a research/action plan related to carefully specified objectives. After this stage, it is basically up to the student to complete the project, unless resource input has been specifically agreed.

The benefits of independent study

Comparisons of the two institutions have enabled the identification of certain core benefits associated with independent study, irrespective of the formal nature of the study. These relate strongly to the development of capabilities. They are concerned both with content issues, 'what students learn', and with process issues, 'how students learn'. Content is not only concerned with knowledge but also with skills development. Process is concerned with how students learn and independent study modules necessarily put emphasis on action learning. The two reinforce each other, so that students acquire both new knowledge and skills and then have the opportunity to test out how they can be applied in a 'real situation' and discover both the extent of their knowledge and abilities and their usefulness.

The nature of learning on an independent study programme facilitates and ensures the development of personal organizational skills. It is unlikely that a student will successfully complete such a module without enhancing such skills. Other core skills acquired include the setting of objectives and the development of measurable criteria relating to the achievement of these objectives. Such modules enable students to experience this process and learn that success depends crucially on such skills. Independent study always requires the improvement of time-management skills by paying explicit attention to the plan for the programme of work and by students being responsible for their own progress in relation to the plan.

Another key attribute which must be developed is self-motivation. All students, whatever their disciplines, are potential managers, and as such need to learn by personal experience the importance of motivational issues to the successful achievement of objectives. Some tutors interpret their role very widely in this area and feel responsible for motivating students. However, this is not usually in the students' long-term interest. Group meetings between students are likely to be more effective, as they encourage 'ownership' of problems. The nature of independent study is such that continual revision and adaptation of the methods and scope of the work is necessary and all this helps develop decision-making skills. Formulating a topic for independent study always requires creativity and developing a method for approaching the issues leads to the development of problem-solving skills.

These represent some of the general skills and competencies developed as a result of taking the independent study modules. In addition, more specific skills associated with each particular undertaking will be developed. The focus of many independent study models frequently encourages the development of a wide range of interpersonal skills. One institution places particular emphasis on the development of an awareness of wider cultural and environmental factors, such as community work, that would normally be encompassed in an academic programme on community work.

Probably of greater significance than developing, acquiring and applying skills and knowledge is the impact of independent study on the entire student experience. It helps students to gain confidence by taking responsibility for their own work and so assists in both their personal and professional development. Much work undertaken in independent study modules prepares students for their working lives by increasing their personal effectiveness.

Conclusion

Independent study allows flexibility and produces benefits which enhance student capabilities. It encourages students to take responsibility for their own work within a rigorous academic environment. It not only builds on knowledge and skills gained elsewhere, but specifically encourages the development of personal qualities and skills which are very useful in future careers. There are a number of academic issues which institutions need to address, particularly the need to balance the desire for innovation and experimentation with the need for academic rigour and external verification. Periodic review of independent study modules and a cross-comparison of experiences between institutions is likely to lead to the enhancement of student experiences by sharing good practice and sharing solutions to identified problems and issues.

Reference

Coventry University (1991) Working Document . . .

Chapter 10

Student Tutoring as a Modular Activity
John Hughes

The problem

The UK has a staying-on rate in full-time 16–18 education and training of less than 50 per cent. If we compare this to our major competitors and consider that in some areas of the UK it is less than 20 per cent, then the problem becomes evident (see Table 10.1) The problem is not confined to the UK, with a similar drop-out problem in many areas of North America. Many of our young people leave education and training at the first available opportunity; they are not aware of the potential benefits of staying on in post-compulsory education and they simply do not see it as something that is relevant or accessible to them. There is an urgent need to increase our participation rates if we are to meet the needs of industry and society as a whole, but also to offer access to education and true equality of opportunity to all of our young people. Science and engineering has a further problem in that children often think of an 'engineer' as someone who works in a dirty factory or a scientist as a mad, balding, boffin.

Table 10.1 *Participation in education and training, percentage of 16–18 year olds (1989)*

	Full-time	Part-time
UK	36	33
Belgium	82	4
Canada	77	-
France	73	8
Germany	49	43
Sweden	73	2
Japan	76	3
USA	75	2
Spain	58	-

Source: UK Department for Education, Government Statistical Service, 15/93, Darlington

Students in many universities and colleges do not get enough opportunities to enhance their problem-solving, organizational and communicational skills. Student tutoring provides an enjoyable and rewarding experience though which students can practise and acquire these skills by working with young people. If electrical engineering undergraduates can explain what electricity is to a 10-year-old then they will probably understand it better themselves!

Towards a solution: student tutoring

Student tutoring involves volunteer students from colleges and universities acting as a resource to the teacher in schools local to their institution. This contact is on a sustained and systematic basis to provide attitudinal gains to student tutor and pupil alike. This contact between college student and school pupil takes place on an in-classroom basis.

In 1990 a project commenced at Imperial College, funded by BP, to which the author was appointed as the BP Fellow for Student Tutoring. The aims of the project at Imperial College were threefold: first, to run and expand the Pimlico Connection at Imperial College; second, to promote the growth of similar schemes across the country; and, third, to undertake research on student tutoring. The second aim led to a massive increase in the number of schemes nationwide from five universities and colleges involved, to 154 by the end of 1993. Many of the 150 new schemes have a component of assessment built into the coursework so that the skills acquired by the student tutors can be recognized. But one of the underlying outcomes in nearly all schemes for both the UK and elsewhere is the provision of positive role-models to children and an attempt to help them with their learning and to provide the college student with capability skills. In all of the schemes in the UK the college is sending its students into local schools for the equivalent of one afternoon a week for between one and three terms. In the student tutoring scheme at Imperial College known as The Pimlico Connection, some 1,300 volunteer students have assisted nearly 15,000 children since 1975. In the academic year 1993/4 there are nearly 200 students active once a week for 15 weeks in 18 local primary and secondary schools with a new initiative with the Science Museum where student *docents* support school visits. One cannot ask, however, for too much altruism and it is heartening to see that in the evaluation (Appendix 2, at the end of this chapter) the overwhelming majority find tutoring fun and enjoyable.

I have always called the following proverb the 'Tutoring Proverb' but in many ways it describes the ethos of capability just as well:

> Tell me, and I forget
>
> Show me, and I remember

Benefits of tutoring

The benefits of running a tutoring scheme are well documented (Hughes, 1992) and are shown in Table 10.2, Appendix 1 and 2. To summarize, students get:

- practice in communication skills;
- insight into how others perceive their subject;
- the satisfaction of doing something useful;
- self-confidence;
- contact with people from different social backgrounds;
- a reinforcement of their subject knowledge.

For their part, pupils not only feel that they learn more, they feel that the lessons are more interesting, enjoyable and easier to follow.

To test the effectiveness of student tutoring on raising school children's aspirations, a small programme took place at Imperial College during the 1991/2 academic year. The study took before and after questionnaires from groups who were tutored for 15 weeks and compared the results to a control group. This provided statistically relevant findings that student tutoring increases the degree to which pupils *try* in science and increases the profile of 'college' as an activity to do when leaving school. The results are summarized in Table 10.2.

Table 10.2 *Years 1979–89 and 1990–91, pupils' opinions*

Percentages of pupils responding: N = 5629
(response rate 5629/8390 = 68%)

	More	About same	Less
Interest of lessons	55	40	4
Ease of following	63	31	4
Enjoyment of lessons	54	38	5
Amount of learning	54	38	5

Student tutoring in the USA

The USA has the longest history of running student tutoring/mentoring schemes. In a national survey carried out in 1990 there were over 1,700 student tutoring/mentoring type schemes in operation across the USA with little differentiation between the terms 'mentoring' and 'tutoring'. The report uses the term 'tutoring and mentoring programmes' to refer to college-sponsored students working with pre-school, elementary or high school pupils to help the pupils improve their academic skills and motivate them to continue their education. In 1988 there were more than 63,000 college students, primarily volunteers, working with nearly 200,000 school pupils with about a third of all colleges involved. The majority of the pupils reported that they acquired increased self-confidence as well as a greater enthusiasm to learn with more self-motivation. The college student tutors reported having an increased commitment to community service, exposure to new cultural environments and improved academic record. Highly structured programmes were found to be the most effective. A second USA survey (Reisner et al., 1990) reports that tutoring and mentoring services have positive effects on:

- test scores, grades, and overall academic performance of disadvantaged elementary and secondary pupils;
- the pupils' motivation and attitude towards education;
- the pupils' familiarity with an environment other than their own;
- the pupils' self-esteem and self-confidence;
- student tutors' leadership and communication skills;
- students' commitment to community service;
- students' self-esteem and self-confidence.

It is Reisner's view (Reisner et al. 1990) that the positive effects are most likely to be demonstrated when there is a high degree of structure to the programme and when the schemes include the following:

- defined time from tutors and mentors (this is often three hours a week);
- systematic screening of prospective tutors and mentors, together with matching with younger pupils;
- thorough training and monitoring of tutors;
- a close relationship between the college and participating schools.

Other international developments

With support from the International Mentoring and Tutoring Project the number of countries running student tutoring schemes continues to rise. This new project developed out of the partnership between Imperial College (University of London) and BP Oil International and involves supporting student tutoring initiatives world-wide as well as BP employee-to-young-people mentoring schemes. The aim, as with the programme in the UK, is to increase the profile of the benefits of education and to provide university and college students with an opportunity of enhancing their transferable skills.

Assessment of student tutoring

Assessment is not a necessary requirement of student tutoring, but every year has seen an increase in the number of schemes which include assessment as part of the student tutor's learning experience. The aim has not been to decide how good an individual is at tutoring, but to identify and formally acknowledge the personal gains acquired by that individual in the course of the tutoring activities.

This interest in assessment has been associated with the developments of personal profiles, National Records of Achievement, Enterprise in Higher Education and the increased recognition by education, industry and commerce of the value of skills such as those concerned with communication, problem-solving and working with others. Furthermore, the introduction of Credit Accumulation Transfer Schemes (CATS) at many institutions has provided enough flexibility for the creation of specific modules in tutoring. In all cases, however, these assessed modules are voluntary options. At no point are students forced to become student tutors.

The objectives for the tutors could be stated as: 'to give FE and HE students the opportunity to develop their social, organizational, leadership, problem-solving and communication skills'. Note that these skills are now part of 'the requirements for work and life' demanded by government, industry and commerce to be included in curricula. These skills are variously described by the following organizations as:

- common skills – Business and Technology Education Council (BTEC)
- common learning outcomes – Confederation of British Industry (CBI)
- core skills – Department for Education (DFE) and General National Vocational Qualifications (GNVQ)
- generic competences – National Vocational Qualifications (NVQ)

Training in these skills can be considered as valuable 'management experience' and may be assessed as part of a management syllabus in vocational courses such as engineering and accountancy. Many of the student tutoring schemes that assess the skills acquired by students do so as part of an academic course in topics ranging from 'The communication of scientific ideas' to 'Education'; the actual student tutoring experience remains voluntary and offers students one of several routes through which they could be assessed. Student tutoring and its assessment could take the equivalent of a brief industrial placement.

The nature of the assessment process will depend on its purpose. Where a qualitative assessment is adequate, the problem is relatively simple as much evidence can be collected in order to match learning outcomes with those listed earlier. It can be valuable to involve students in selecting which methods of assessment will be used. This could be carried out by showing some of the BP tutor training video and then brainstorming to allow the students to generate the assessment criteria and thus 'own' them. An overall marking plan might include evidence collected using the following methods:

- self-assessment
- portfolio
- observed performance
- written documentation: log book
- written documentation: report
- oral presentation.

There is a chapter on assessment in the BP resource pack that gives much more detail.

Help in starting a tutoring scheme

BP has supported the production of a comprehensive set of resources to support new schemes. If you would like a copy of the free booklet on tutoring write to: BP Educational Service, PO Box 934, Poole, Dorset, BH17 7BR, UK. Tel: 0202 669940, Fax 0202 679326. They can also provide information on the resource pack, training video, handbill and posters.

References

Hughes, J (1992) *Happiest Moments at Imperial: Pimlico Connection 17th Annual Report*, London: Imperial College.

Resiner, E, Petrie, C and Armitage, M (1990) *A Review of Progress Involving College Students as Tutors and Mentors in Grades K–12*, Washington DC: Policy Studies Institute.

Appendix 1: teachers' opinions, 1979-1989

Teacher responses: N = 186 (response rate 186/301 = 62%).

With tutors	Easier to handle	More difficult to handle	About the same as usual
lessons were	63	6	26

	More enjoyable	Less enjoyable	About the same as usual
teaching was	70	2	23

	More than usual	Less than usual	About as much as usual
pupils seemed to learn	69	3	25

Appendix 2: tutors' opinions

Percentages of students indicating that they thought they had benefited from being a tutor in the ways listed: 1991-92 response rate 97/128 = 76% (1979–1989 and 1990–91 response rate 633/918 = 69%)

By reinforcing your knowledge of some aspect of your subject?

Greatly	8 (3)	Not at all	48(56)
Somewhat	41(38)	Not sure	2 (3)

By getting practice in the simple communication of scientific ideas?

Greatly	52(55)	Not at all	4 (2)
Somewhat	43 (40)	Not sure	1 (2)

By gaining insight into how other people perceive your subject?

Greatly	29(35)	Not at all	15(10)
Somewhat	55(52)	Not sure	1 (3)

By increasing your self-confidence?

Greatly	31(17)	Not at all	13(18)
Somewhat	39(43)	Not sure	3(6)

By getting to know something about people with a different social background to your own?

Greatly	52(39)	Not at all	5(14)
Somewhat	39(43)	Not sure	4 (4)

By feeling that you were doing something useful with what you had already learned?

Greatly	63(49)	Not at all	3 (6)
Somewhat	32(43)	Not sure	2 (4)

Did the tutoring interfere with your college studies?

Greatly	3 (1)	Not at all	66(62)
Somewhat	29(29)	Not sure	1 (7)

Do you feel that you acted as a positive role model to the tutees to learn about post-education?

Greatly	17	Not at all	17
Somewhat	51	Not sure	16

Chapter 11

Crediting Students for Helping Students

David Longworth

The context

At the University of Central Lancashire the majority of undergraduate teaching takes place within a Credit Accumulation and Transfer Scheme (CATS). The author's place within this is currently as the subject leader for geography, responsible, amongst other things, for academic development. Because of the nature of our geography courses and of the world of graduate employment, it is essential that we teach basic skills in information technology to all our first year students. Experience has clearly shown that this is best achieved via small-group teaching with a high requirement of 'hands-on' practice. However, the well-known pressures of increasing student intakes and declining per-capita resources have strongly militated against this. The problem thus faced was how to teach the basic IT skills in small practical groups without substantial amounts of staff class-contact time.

Given that a considerable number of our students are considering entering teaching careers in due course, a potential solution was seen in providing a small pedagogical course for students who already have considerable knowledge and skill in the use of IT within geography, and giving credit within their degree programmes for assisting with the teaching of the first-year practicals. A successful bid for 'Enterprise' funding freed sufficient time for the author to develop these ideas and put them into practice on an experimental basis. Without this funding, the development would not have been possible, given current workloads within the department in which the teaching is required.

The course

Two important concepts underlying this development are those of integration and interaction. Two course units were envisaged simultaneously: one to teach first-year students basic information technology in relation to first-year undergraduate geography, the other to teach second/third-year students some introductory pedagogical skills. The teaching unit was envisaged as assisting in the teaching and development of the geographic knowledge, the geography seen as providing the context for the development of pedagogic skills. These relationships have been found to be quite successful during the first year of operation, though integration within the geography course needs to be improved.

The specific course objectives are:

- Teaching information technology to first-year undergraduate geographers:
  - to overcome the technophobia present in many students;
  - to demonstrate the relevance of IT to undergraduate study in general and geography in particular;
  - to form a sound basis for transferable IT skills development for undergraduate and vocational purposes, by inculcating sufficient keyboard skills, network- and software-familiarity to ensure smooth progression to second-year practical courses.
- Teaching second- and third-year students how to teach IT skills to first-year students:
  - to provide a 'testing ground' or 'learner pool' for students interested in pursuing a teaching career;
  - to develop skills in classroom awareness and effective communication;
  - to develop skills in curriculum development and evaluation;
  - to develop skills in assessment design and implementation;
  - to build teamwork skills.

Overall, the development is closely related to the recommendations of the Higher Education Branch of the Employment Department (Employment Department, 1992). The relationship to those recommendations is that:

- it seeks to develop transferable skills;
- it could not achieve its potential without Enterprise funding;
- staff development would occur through the project leader's involvement and his or her dissemination of results;
- it seeks to embed IT within the subject matter of the student's main subject
- the skills teaching in IT is closely linked to institutional policy, and all necessary hardware, plus most necessary software was previously available.

The course in IT assumes no previous knowledge of computer systems, keyboards or software. Great attention is given to staging the work in clear unambiguous language, avoiding unnecessary computer jargon. Course content ranges from an introduction to the basic university hardware and the relevant terminology, through login, password and menu operations, to familiarization with software and induction to its applications. Word-processing, database, spreadsheet and graphics operations are developed through Microsoft Works, statistical analysis introduced in Minitab (including some basic graphs), graphical sophistication is achieved via EXCEL, and modelling via Model Builder. The students are in class for one hour per week and the course is rated at two credits to allow for necessary follow-up work.

Teaching is undertaken in groups of 10 to 18 students, in which each student works through carefully sequenced task sheets under the supervision of one or two second- or third-year student teachers, ideally not exceeding a teacher: student ratio of 1:12. Hence a group of 16 students would have two student teachers in support.

The task sheets are more than staged instructions, requiring students to record their responses to various questions about the software capabilities and applications. To maximize the efficiency of the task sheets as the major teaching vehicle, a cycle of design and evaluation has been developed. The feedback referred to in the third-level loop in Figure 11.1 is derived from two perspectives: the regular team meetings of student-teachers and course tutor provide information from the teaching perspective, and questionnaires and informal conversations provide information from the learning perspective. These are also encouraged to be interactive. The whole process is very time-consuming, but once the work is complete, the classes run well, and future modification is likely to be minimal. A fourth-level evaluation is envisaged as the focus of a special project undertaken by one of the student teachers, which will make recommendations for task sheet design and use for 1993/4.

The pedagogical course unit includes direction on class preparation, organization and evaluation. Each student teacher is responsible for supervision of one practical group for one hour per week. Regular team meetings are designed to deal pragmatically with real-life issues as they arise, and put these issues into the broader context of the pedagogical literature. Through team meetings the student teachers have become involved in the design of parts of the pieces of work set for the assessment of 'their' students. The student-teachers are required to keep personal logbooks of their experience, including observations and evaluations within the classroom and records of discussions in team meetings. These logbooks form 50 per cent of the assessment of the student-teachers, and act as the springboard for an investigation and report regarding one aspect of the course relating practice and principle. The report forms the other 50 per cent of the student-teacher assessment. The student-teachers have responded well to their responsibilities, working nicely as a team and showing considerable commitment to 'their' students. In January 1993, two student-teachers attended the annual conference of the Institute of British Geographers to support a poster presentation on the scheme, benefiting enormously from the experience and stimulating considerable interest amongst participants.

Evaluation and conclusion

Having completed about two-thirds of the course, over 78 per cent of first-year students returning questionnaires (40 per cent response rate) report that they are pleased with their progress and do not feel they could have

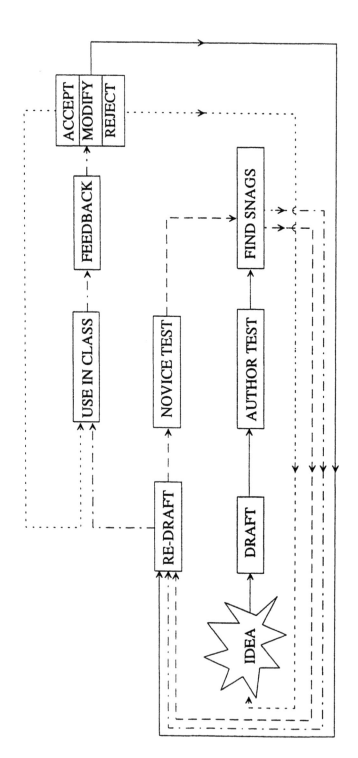

Figure 11.1 *Information technology IT tasksheets, cycle of design and evaluation*

achieved more in a course of this nature. While the disadvantages identified in student feedback were only commented on by a few, they need to be taken seriously. One student-teacher has now prepared a detailed report on the matter of clarity and ambiguity, making recommendations for rewording or restructuring of the task sheets for the following year. The perception that some of the work is too simple or patronizing presents a more difficult problem. This largely relates to the fact that the course assumes no previous experience of computers, yet attracts some students who are not rank beginners. As with many courses, particularly those which are skill-based, the setting of the entry level and the exit level is critical. In this case, we must set the entry level low to cater for the majority of our students. The exit level is specifically related to two criteria: what can be achieved by one hour per week in class plus one hour per week follow-up by the majority of students: and what entry level is required for smooth progression into the second-year course unit in practical investigation procedures, which demands considerable development of computer skills. These levels, and the intervening teaching can be symbolized in Figure 2, a model developed by the author, substantially adapting a model presented by Hazari (1991). Whilst it is clear that a few students, mainly drawn from the mature cohort in the course, have for example, keyboard and word processing skills, they cannot be exempted because they are unfamiliar with our hardware and software systems, and with the subject-specific content of the Geography with which the course is integrated.

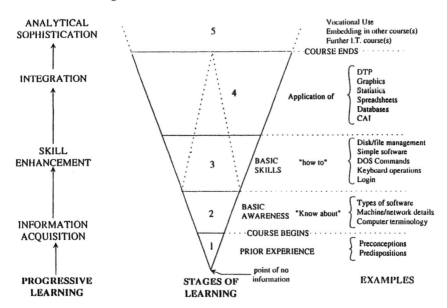

Figure 11.2 *A model for I.T. course construction*

Some student-teachers and their students have suggested streaming the groups to enable faster or greater progress of those with some previous experience. This has been rejected partly because of timetabling difficulties and more particularly because greater differentials were already under discussion in the student-teacher team meetings, which suggested utilizing the existing knowledge and skills of the students to assist those who were finding the greatest need for one-to-one support. This is now the favoured technique to go some way to resolving an otherwise intractable problem. It is possible that it is in this context that interest and ability may develop so far as to produce the emergent cohort of prospective student-teachers for subsequent years.

The first-year students' evaluation of the use of student-teachers so far has been most encouraging. No student has reported being badly served by any student-teacher: the only negative comment (made by only two or three students) is that at times more student-teachers would be useful. Reported advantages are several and have the support of considerable consensus. The advantages identified are included in such comments as 'It's good to be taught by someone who only one or two years ago was where we are now', and 'They are easier to talk to; we don't feel stupid asking simple questions.' Substantial appreciation is apparent in statements like, 'They are extremely approachable and helpful', 'It's an excellent method', and 'I can't praise the student-teacher enough'. The student teachers themselves have expressed enthusiasm for the scheme, identifying insight into the practice of teaching, development of communication and teamwork skills, and engagement in 'real-world' practical activities as particularly valuable attributes.

Based on this experience, the author believes that student-teachers could become a valuable resource in limited contexts where the focus is on basic skills, and where they can be adequately supported by experienced teaching staff. It is imperative that the student-teacher's work should contribute substantially to their personal development in ways which are relevant to their degree and career programmes, and that all arrangements are transacted with the utmost integrity. That a modular course can credit the students' work enables the institution to resource the course and to validate and value what students contribute to and learn from the course. This approach should not be seen as an easy route to cheap teaching. It isn't.

References

Employment Department (1992) 'Enterprise in Higher Education: Information Technology within EHE' (a discussion paper) London: Higher Education Branch, Department of Employment.

Chapter 12

Accrediting Students for Extracurricular Learning

Graham Gaskell and Sarah Brierley

Introduction

Two-thirds of a university student's waking hours are devoted to activities other than attending class or studying. When asked about their most meaningful learning experiences in higher education, former students frequently report that out-of-class experiences increased their competence and self-assurance – qualities that are important to personal satisfaction and professional success (Kuh *et al.*, 1991). As three recent graduates we felt strongly that some form of credit should be given for the learning that occurs outside courses. Within our institution, Oxford Brookes University, we have been able to shape university policies to achieve this aim. Two of us (Brookes and Gaskell) have done this through our role as Coordinator for Student Enterprise, one of us (Brierley) as President of the Student Union. This chapter describes how we have developed a module (with many similarities to the independent study modules described in Chapter 9 of this volume by Murray and Gore) to give academic credit for three broad areas of experience. These are:

- student representative/student union work;
- work within the local community;
- individual work experience (ie, work experience not attached to a specific course or qualification).

Why credit students for extracurricular activities?

In arguing a case for giving academic credit for extracurricular activities we will advance three arguments: that extracurricular activities provide valuable learning opportunities, that the pressures of the modular course and financial hardship discourage involvement in extracurricular activities, and that the three areas identified are particularly worthy of support and will benefit the university.

Extracurricular activities provide valuable learning opportunities

Fortunately we were swimming with a strong tide. Changes in recent years have led to increasing importance being attached to the acquisition of transferable skills while at university, and the Higher Education Council (HEFC) have made it clear that quality should be measured in terms of the *totality* of the student learning experience. Emphasis seems to have been shifting from credentials to competences – what students can do rather than what qualifications they obtain.

At our own institution, following a long process of consultation, five major categories of transferable skills (learning skills, communication, self-management, team work and problem solving) have been defined, and it has been agreed that all disciplines should ensure these are embedded within their courses. However, if students are to be fully aware of the transferability of the skills and the knowledge they acquire within their academic subject areas, we believe they will need to find opportunities and contexts elsewhere to demonstrate and practise their learning.

Second, although many teaching staff are moving away from traditional methods of 'spoon-fed' teaching and beginning to emphasize active learning methods, many courses will have little experience of encouraging the development of the skills associated with self-management. These are precisely the skills which are commonly encouraged and fostered by involvement in the three areas identified above. At present these experiences undoubtedly enhance a student's personal development, though understanding these developments is more difficult as at present there are no opportunities to reflect upon or articulate them.

The pressures of the modular course and financial hardship discourage involvement in extracurricular activities

The nature of the modular course, with exams for most students at the end of every term and coursework throughout, requires that students work consistently hard in their years at Oxford Brookes. At the same time, particularly in an area of high-cost housing, increasing numbers of students are suffering acute financial hardship. Working part-time (and in some cases practically full-time) has become a necessity for many students to ensure that they can remain at college. Mature students – another rapidly growing section of the student community – may have family commitments putting pressure on their time. The consequence of these effects combined has been to reduce the numbers of students involved in unpaid extracurricular activities. Many simply don't feel they can spare the time.

Recent research into the effects of part-time work on students' academic performance has shown conclusively that marks are lower for students with term-time employment (Paton and Lindsay, 1994). Devising a module to give credit for the learning taking place in many of these jobs (clearly some are so monotonous, undemanding and unskilled as to provide virtually no learning opportunities) would clearly help many students.

The three areas identified are particularly worthy of support and will benefit the university

As it appears that the module we have developed will be marginally more expensive (or 'resource-intensive' in the jargon of academic committees!) in terms of staff time than an ordinary module, we've seen the need to develop arguments other than 'this is good for the students'. It is a happy coincidence, therefore, that encouraging involvement in these activities will also benefit the university.

Student representatives sitting on course and central university commit-tees are essential to ensuring effective quality assurance, as the HEFC has recognized. Doing this job properly – gauging student views on their courses and any proposed changes, attending meetings, learning the necessary committee skills and academic acronyms and jargon – requires considerable time and effort. At present, student representatives receive little formal recognition from staff or students for their responsibilities, and may feel under-valued by the institution. Crediting the learning which takes place would encourage students to take the role more seriously. If, as many believe, one of the key purposes of education is about empowering students for life, students' unions encourage this better than almost any other part of our institutions. However, those officers find their time, effort and learning completely unrewarded; indeed, most find their studies suffer and receive lower grades.

The huge expansion of higher education in recent years has put increasing strain on relations between universities and surrounding local commu-nities. At the same time, as we noted earlier, financial hardship has led to lower involvement in community and charity work. Giving academic credit for the learning that occurs in these projects and organizations should enable more students to participate in such activities, while simultaneously improving relations with the local communities.

At first sight, the advantage to the university of having more students involved in work placements, or receiving credit for part-time employment, may seem less obvious. Some academics still seem to regard dialogue with employers as irrelevant and treat suggestions for closer links with deep hostility. However, we believe there can be clear benefits of such linkages. Few of today's undergraduates go on to specialist research; *they go out to seek employment in a rapidly changing, competitive world*. If (non-vocational) academic studies are to better prepare undergraduates with the skills and knowledge to enable them to find enjoyable work, they need to be aware of the changes and developments in the requirements of employers and the worlds outside the university.

How to do it

Our modular course requires students to pass 18 advanced module credits to obtain an honours degree (27 modules if it is a four-year course). Of these it is possible for students to take two modules that are unrelated to their subjects of study. Each subject or field has an 'independent study' module allowing a student to study subjects not covered or to look at a particular area in greater depth. The independent study module can act as a vehicle for crediting students for extracurricular activities in some instances, but as many subject groups require it to be directly related to their subject area, this restricts many students from receiving such credits.

Therefore, an independent study module that is unattached to any field or subject would overcome such a limitation and enable students to gain credit for such work. We set about trying to devise such a module. Our first attempt was to suggest the model shown in Figure 12.1.

The basic template learning contract would have sub-sections for the various types of activity as shown in Figure 12.1. The learning contract for these would then be negotiated by the tutor and the student on an individual basis. The contract will include:

- the nature of the experience;
- the time required;
- the description of tasks, learning objectives and skills;
- the learning outcomes;
- evidence for assessment;
- tutor and/or mentor (if involved) support.

However, although this model would clearly allow for flexibility, it initially looked as if there would be problems caused by the learning outcomes and evidence for assessment being negotiated wholly on an individual basis.

Fortunately, at this point, one of us attended a one-day conference disseminating the results of a project entitled 'Work-based learning for academic credit' carried out by Chester College of HE, the University of

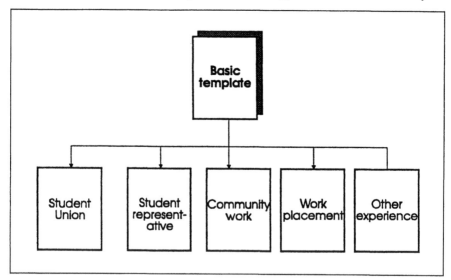

Figure 12.1 *Unattached independent study module mechanics*

Liverpool and Liverpool John Moores University. Although this project differed from our own – it gives credit solely for the area of work placements – the defined learning outcomes required little alteration and were closely linked to a tested, successful assessment regime. Based on their experience, we have adopted the following learning outcomes and assessment criteria:

- **Learning outcomes**
  There will be six learning outcomes:
  (a) Knowledge of what an organization/committee does.
  (b) Understanding of how an organization achieves its aims with reference to its internal organization and management
  or understanding of how the committee achieves its aims with reference to its relationship to and with other committees and management.
  (c) Understanding of the economic/environmental context and its inter-action with the organization;
  or understanding of the issues of concern to students which are relevant to the particular committee.
  (d) The acquisition of transferable skills.
  (e) The ability to evaluate experiential learning in the light of:
     – skills and subject knowledge gained within courses
     – subject knowledge and skills gained directly from the experience
     – knowledge gained from the supporting programme
     – the students' own independent sources.
  (f) The ability to reflect on and evaluate learning from the experience as a whole.

- **Assessment**
  There will be four methods of assessing the learning outcomes:
  – presentations
  – dialogue assessment
  – portfolio
  – evaluation document.

Presentations will take two forms: The first, in weeks 4, 5 or 6, will be of 15 minutes' duration and give particular scope for learning outcomes (a), (b) and (c). The second, in weeks 9 or 10, will also be of 15 minutes' duration and give particular scope for learning outcomes (d) and (e).

The *dialogue assessment* will be an ongoing process of reporting back by the student with, in particular, a more formal meeting being held after each presentation.

The *portfolio* will contain an account of the students' experience written as a learning diary. It will include details of any specific assignments completed, and would normally be within the range of 4,000 to 5,000 words.

The *evaluation document* will take the form of a concise, structured report of the students' views of the extent of their achievement of the learning outcomes, particularly learning outcome (f). It must be typed and must not exceed 1,500 words.

Supporting and resourcing the module

Assigning resources such as funding and staff has caused initial difficulties because the module will not come under a school title (ie, business, languages, etc). It will be slightly more expensive than traditional modules, as there is greater one-to-one contact between staff and students, but should 'cost less' than other independent study modules as some support will be available to students through group meetings with others working within the same broad areas.

Opposition to the module

As we presented our proposals in discussions and at formal committees, initially there was much opposition from teaching staff to giving academic credit for involvement in extracurricular activities which focused around two arguments. The first is the immediate response of many lecturers, put simply, 'This is not academic'. Well, that depends upon what we all mean by 'academic'. It is unlikely that this activity will fit neatly into one academic discipline but to do the work effectively requires the development of knowledge and skills. As the debate within the university has moved on, the support for the module has increased as we have learnt to emphasize that the credit is not for the experience itself but for the reflection and the assessment of the learning that has been developed out of that experience.

The second and more serious concern is that crediting this involvement will alter the motives of students choosing to stand as course representatives, etc. There is no easy answer to this - indeed, it remains one of our concerns. We hope and believe it will make little difference to the types of students attracted to these areas, as what is proposed is not an easy opinion, though clearly this is something that will need to be reviewed after the university has learned from the experience of accrediting this activity. We hope the first limited experiment with the module will be in summer term 1993/4.

Conclusion

This chapter has focused on our experience at Oxford Brookes. It is clear, however, that universities elsewhere in Britain are debating and devising (or have devised) similar schemes to accredit learning which occurs outside the classroom.

We are also aware that in many American universities there is greater discussion and recognition of these 'extracurricula' activities. Indeed the term 'extracurricula' devalues this experience, this learning. In certain American colleges the preferred term is 'co-curricular activities', to demonstrate that this learning has equal value to the traditional classroom and discipline-based curriculum. One study of the American college curriculum (Gaff, 1991) argues:

If the curriculum and co-curricular aspects of college life were joined more closely, the college experience would be more coherent and students would have a better and more holistic education. Because so much more can be done on this front at most institutions this remains an agenda for the future.

We hope that we have helped our institution to make limited but significant progress to this end, and we believe that this and similar developments elsewhere are a significant way in which modular courses can aid student capability.

References

Gaff, J (1991) *New Hope for the College Curriculum*, San Francisco, CA: Jossey Bass.Kuh, G *et al.* (1991) *Involving Colleges*, San Francisco, CA: Jossey Bass.

Kuh, G, Schuh, J H and Whitte, E J (1991) *Involving Colleges*, San Francisco, CA: Jossey Bass.

Paton, R and Lindsay, R (1994) *The Effect of Paid Employment on the Academic Performance of Full-Time Students in Higher Education*, Oxford: Oxford Brookes University.

Chapter 13

An Institutional Policy for Course Development Through Learning Outcomes
Mike Vaughan and Harvey Woolf

Introduction: rationale and principles

The University of Wolverhampton currently has some 19,000 students studying on one or more of its five campuses in the Black Country and Shropshire or as off-site learners in this country or overseas. The whole of its undergraduate provision, including many of its HND awards, is organized on a semesterized modular basis which allows students considerable amount of flexibility in designing their study programmes, even in specialist or single-subject degrees. One method of providing students with more explicit rationales with which to design their modular programmes is to write modules in terms of the learning outcomes. This was recognized in the-then Polytechnic's 1992/3 strategic plan and the learning outcomes project was established to explore ways of implementing this commitment to formulating the learning undertaken by students in terms of its outcomes.

The introduction of learning outcomes is consistent with other of the university's educational and ideological objectives because an outcomes curriculum will:

- clarify for both students and staff the knowledge, theory and skills to be developed in modules;

- commit module tutors to ensuring that the achievement of the module's tasks and purposes are facilitated;
- demystify the processes of assessment for students by articulating clear goals;
- facilitate claims for credit from learning achieved in other contexts, the Accreditation of Prior Experiential Learning (APEL);
- allow the easy development of strategies to replicate learning outside the university, for example, in the workplace;
- serve as a basis on which to address the relationship with higher-level NVQs;
- assist in the overall monitoring of the quality of the learning process.

In addition to these institutional purposes, the project saw itself as a broader staff development exercise by encouraging detailed, collaborative reflection on the nature and purposes of subjects in the university curriculum.

This chapter first describes the development of the project from its inception in autumn 1992, up to December 1993, and then identifies some of the key issues generated by the process. As two project managers, we recognize that this account inevitably misses the dialectical cut and thrust of debate that took place within the module teams working at subject level. It was in those contexts among subject experts that many of the doubts, scepticism and false starts were explored. Thus, though aware of any tensions and uncertainties in the writing of the modules, we essentially dealt with completed drafts and with subject representatives. This perhaps led us to underestimate the difficulties some module writers and subject representatives had. It did, however, allow us to retain a strategic overview.

The development of the project

The primary goals of the project were to (re)write up to six modules in the September to December of the autumn term 1992 and to produce guidelines on writing learning outcomes that would replace the existing university content-focused module descriptions. The project was based on the assumptions that guidelines would be:

- produced by a central team of teachers and academic administrators;
- tested at subject/course/award validation events;
- modified in the light of the experience of both the validation and, more importantly, the operation of the modules.

Thus staff and curriculum development would run in parallel, be iterative and incremental.

The university's current organization, which gives subject groups the responsibility for developing modules, defined the scope of the project. Each of seven schools (departments), in discussion with the project managers, nominated one subject group to write or rewrite six modules in terms of learning outcomes. These were to be distributed across each of the three undergraduate levels of study to enable the group to address issues of progression.

Because it was thought likely that there would be common issues, and that inter-subject debate would be valuable in the pilot phase, each subject group nominated an individual to 'represent' the subject in the project and a core group was formed to focus discussion, act as a sounding board and in general progress the project. Above all, it was clear from the Unit for the Development of Adult Continuing Education (UDACE) project on learning outcomes (Otter, 1991, 1992) that a key issue in adopting this process was how to constitute the central team. It was critical that the development was owned by the subjects and their staff rather than being imposed by a group of 'professional' curriculum developers divorced from the classroom, laboratory or fieldwork. In the event, we selected participants on the basis of:

- their work hitherto on outcomes and related areas, eg Enterprise in HE projects, BTEC;
- known staff expertise/commitment;
- range of types of subject, including those with emergent NVQ standards;
- receptivity to curriculum change/design.

This produced the following group:

Subject	Number of modules written/rewritten
Biochemistry	6
Computing (systems analysis)	3
Construction (surveying)	3
Education studies	6
Engineering systems	3
Health studies	6
Human resource management	6
Philosophy	6
Statistics	3

In the light of the UDACE project's experience, our commitment to a pragmatic rather than previously theorized approach, and the heterogeneity of the group, we did not attempt to specify either what the outcomes should be or how they should be formulated and presented. Our intention was to allow these specifications to emerge from reading, discussion among the group and with external contributors and from each member of staff working on her or his modules. We consciously eschewed the language of competence because we wanted the team to think beyond the occupational functionalism of, for example, NVQs.

In the first instance the group was supplied with relevant current literature and brief introductory seminars, while identifying with their parent subject groups the modules to be addressed. The core group met initially fortnightly and then weekly, to consider issues which had arisen in the subject area and to compare solutions, review developing documentation and agree on common approaches where appropriate. Finally the group debated and agreed the common format for the presentation of the modules to be adopted for submission to a university validation panel in May 1993. A sample module in this format appears in the Appendix at the end of this chapter.

The validation event viewed the project positively, recommending that the model that had been developed should be adopted institutionally with any amendments deriving from the evaluation of the modules run in 1993/4. A second phase will begin in January 1994 which will review the experience of the first tranche of modules taught, explore assessment issues and extend outcomes to additional subjects. In short, we see this as a ripple approach to both curriculum and staff development.

Key issues

The key issues fall into two broad categories: those relating to the management of a development project, and those relating to the substantive debates raised by an outcomes-led curriculum.

Management

- Although we would continue to argue that the pragmatic approach is one appropriate for a diverse group, we now think that it would be desirable to produce a model (or models) on which the team can work immediately, rather than starting with a general discussion of the methodology and asking the group to devise their own model. This is particularly so if working in as short a timetable as ours.
- If theoretical material is used early on, it needs to be carefully structured and even edited to ensure that it is accessible to all participants and not only those already versed in curriculum development.
- External contributions may be most effective if they come later rather than earlier so that participants can use them as expert witnesses instead of as 'briefers' on the project.
- Introducing small group working early would improve the support that the group offers to individuals.
- There is a need to meet not just regularly but frequently to ensure continuity of dialogue.
- Even for a pilot, a longer lead time than three months is necessary.
- In the development phase, it would be useful to use existing 'expert' staff as mentors for staff new to outcomes.

Curriculum

What happens to syllabus content? If describing modules in terms of outcomes necessarily meant jettisoning content/knowledge in favour of skills, competences and capabilities, then a number of participants, particularly those with professional bodies to satisfy, were concerned that these modules would lose academic credibility.

To meet this challenge, the group decided to reformulate the NCVQ concept of a *range statement*. This was especially controversial because range statements were seen by some as carrying with them the ideology of occupational performance, which is currently defined by NVQ Levels 1 to 3. Therefore our reformulation incorporated and made explicit the role of knowledge and theory in demonstrating academic competence. This approach allowed the range statement to be used to define either particular areas of a subject within which the specified knowledge would be demonstrated or the methods of enquiry to be practised. This enables the range statement to be used as the syllabus component of a module.

Our broader definition of range statement not only operationalized the outcomes in terms of knowledge and theory but also proved to be the primary link between the specified outcomes for each module and their assessment. Further, the range statement is a primary determinant of the level of assessment tasks and therefore of the level of the module. Certainly, the initial impressions of the students taking the validated modules indicate that they welcome the explicitness and clarity of modules described in outcomes and range statements, not least because staff have formally focused students on the outcomes to be achieved at and by each teaching session.

Framework for assessment

A major requirement of a learning outcomes approach is that there should be explicit linkage between the assessment schedule and the outcomes defined. There is, no doubt, a risk that such a linkage will restrict development and innovation in assessment. Yet the converse risk – that students are not clear what is expected of them – seems to us more serious. The compromise reached has been that for any iteration the assignment of outcomes to components of the assessment must be made clear and adhered to, though properly agreed changes can be made in subsequent iterations.

Since modular structures tend to over-assess, assessment planning for students can only be facilitated by disturbing assessment workloads across the module. This informed the discussion of the patterns of assessment. We therefore agreed the approximate number of outcomes we would seek to assess and chose to bundle outcomes into groups rather than identify key outcomes or sequence them. 'Bundling' was linked to forms of assessment as well as outcome coherence, and included personal competences.

As the bundle was to be the essential element of assessment, it was decided that students must pass all bundles. However, it was not necessary for all outcomes in each bundle to be passed since it was thought that some outcomes could be more significant than others. Bundle criteria will specify what grade profile or range of passes will be required to pass the bundle. Bundling also reopened the discussion on what constitutes the achievement of appropriate learning prerequisites for the next level of study. Evidently, with a learning outcomes approach, there may well be no need to require students to pass the whole module to continue to the subsequent module(s).

All of these are without doubt contentious matters and will certainly be revisited in the next phase of the project.

An often-repeated concern was how the achievement by students of unexpected outcomes can be given due weight. While there is no easy answer, there seems to us to be no problem in principle in identifying an 'unanticipated' element through the assessment regime. Rather, we think the difficulty may be in conceptualizing precisely the ways in which such an outcome might be valued.

In general, detailed grading criteria were seen by most of the group as a downstream activity. Emphasis tended to be placed on the types of assessment to be used. We suspect that this difference from the UDACE project team view derives from our starting with small discrete elements of programmes which we think can easily be locked into learning and assessment processes. It must also be said that the timescale was such that the detailed work on assessment was only beginning when the project finished. Subsequent comment from staff has suggested that this linkage is an important determinant of teaching style in delivery.

Personal competences

The debate about personal competences and the extent to which they should be identified as formal outcomes which should be assessed informed much of the work of the group, at both subject and project levels. What was noticeable at the latter was the amount of common ground shared by all subjects and the way in which the competences were deployed throughout all modules. The Department of Employment's Personal Competence Model provided a useful tool for specifying such competences. (The model was trailed by nine higher education institutions in 1991/2 under the direction of Sue Otter. At the time of writing the results of the project remain unpublished.)

The incorporation of personal competences into module outcomes therefore required module writers to create forms of assessment which could carry personal competence assessment as part of an integrated assessment package and to articulate the relevant personal competences as module outcomes. This would help students to select modules which either restricted or widened the range of personal competences they wanted to acquire.

The issue of how to record such competences is still under discussion, as is how, if at all, to grade them. One solution would be to include them as part of a record of achievement. In turn this prompts another, as yet, unresolved, question: how can (and should) opportunities to demonstrate personal competences be distributed across a total student programme which is disaggregated into modules? The integrated course approach to specifying outcomes resolves this in a particular way not necessarily available in a more permeable system.

Concluding observations

We are sure that writing modules in terms of learning outcomes clarifies the purposes of a module for everyone involved, be they students, tutors, academic advisers, APEL applicants or employers. Despite the benefits there are barriers to the development of an outcome-based curriculum. The question of whether occupational functional analysis can be applied to academic processes raises the issue whether academic work is in any real sense distinctive. We believe that specifying the capabilities we expect our graduates to possess as a result of taking our awards can be achieved and that describing learning outcomes provides a different lodestar from the traditional syllabus for students on modular programmes.

Our experience confirmed that diverse disciplines contributing to modular programmes have more in common than they think. This and the other issues we have identified are perhaps obvious and have already been signalled by UDACE but, as with so much learning, it is only by doing that we recognized the full import of the experiences of others. That is as true of tutors as it is of students.

Our thanks go to the following colleagues who did the real work on the project and who have provided us with so much stimulus over the past months: Jo Allan (education studies), Ray Bins (statistics), Jane Edis (administrative support), Jenny Gilbert (computing), Nigel leighton (engineering), Sarah Luft (health science), Ken Norton (biochemistry), Lynnette Priddey (human resource management), John Ratcliffe (construction), Carol Smith (administrative support), and Bruce Young (philosophy).

References

Otter, S (1991) *What Can Graduates Do?*, London: UDACE and the Department of Employment.
Otter, S (1992) *Learning Outcomes in Higher Education*, London: UDACE and the Department of Employment.

Appendix 1: Example of module description written in learning outcomes

Note: This description has been submitted for internal validation. At present it does not include a fully developed assessment criteria or schedule.

MODULE TITLE   Introductory Biochemistry

SCHOOL   Applied Science

MODULE LEADER   Dr K Norton

LEVEL   1

CREDIT VALUE   15

DURATION   One Semester

SUBJECT BOARD   Chemistry/Biochemistry

EXTERNAL EXAMINER Professor K Brocklehurst

PARENT & OTHER COURSE PROGS

BSc Biochemistry
Others BSc Applied Sciences, BSc Applied Chemistry, BSc Biomedical Sciences, BSc Environmental Science, BSc Biological Sciences, MODDS.

PREREQUISITES   'A' level chemistry or Foundation Chemistry (CH116)

CO-REQUISITES   None

EXCLUDED MODULE COMBINATIONS   None

LEARNING OUTCOMES/RANGE STATEMENTS

01   Relate chemical principles to the structure of biological building block molecules   Structured questions in test 1 and test 2

Range of application
Nucleosides and nucleotides
Amino Acids
Monosaccharides, trioses, pentoses, hexoses lipids, triglycerides, phosphoglycerides.

02   Derive the structure of biological macromolecules and structures from building block molecules   Structured questions in test 1 and test 2

Range of application
Base pairing and DNA
Types of RNA
Proteins and peptides
Storage and structural polysaccharides
Membranes and liposomes.

03   Relate the structure of biological   Assignment
      macromolecules to their biological   problem 1
      function.

Range of application
DNA and transcriptions in protein synthesis
mRNA, tRNA and translation in protein
synthesis
Proteins as examples of enzymes, structural
proteins, carrier proteins antibodies
Carbohydrates as energy sources and in the
form of glycoproteins
Membranes, fluidity and transport processes

04   Explain the key role of enzymes in   Assignment
      metabolism.   problem 2

Range of application
Nomenclature and classification of
metabolic enzymes
Specificity of enzymes
Mechanism of action of enzymes
Effect of pH and temperature on enzyme action
Qualitative distinction between Michaelis
Menton and ailosteric enzyme
Qualitative distinction between competitive
and non competitive inhibition.

05   Draw and use overview metabolic chart to   Structured
      demonstrate links between major   questions in
      metabolic pathways.   test 2

Range of application
Carbohydrate metabolism
Amino acid metabolism
Fatty acid metabolism.

06   Explain how carbohydrate are synthesized   Structured
      from CO_2 by means of the C_3 and C_4 questions
      pathways.   in test 2

Range of application
Role of pigments
Synthesis and role of $NADPH_2$ and ATP
Factors affecting the rate of C_3 pathway.

07   Use detailed instructions to acquire   Practical
      a range of core biochemical practical   results and
      skills and cognate techniques.   reports

Range of application
Separation techniques, salting out,
TLC, ion exchange, gel filtration
Construct calibration curves for given assays
Assay protein and glucose concentration
Measure rate of an enzyme catalysed reaction.

08	Use computer enzyme simulation packages	Observation and practical reports

Range of applications
Plan experimental investigation
Interpret results and calculate
biochemical parameters.

09	Manipulate experimental data to calculate biochemical parameters in the absence of an inhibitor.	Question in test 2

Range of application
Specific activity of an enzyme K_m
and V_{max} for an enzyme.

10	Use IT packages to present given data and date from practical exercises in specified visual form.	Practical

Range of application
Graphs
Bar Charts
Word processed reports.

011	Communicate scientific data and understanding of scientific principles by written and oral means.	Practical and tutorials

Range of application
Practical reports
Discussion groups.

012	Demonstrate safe working practice and hazard analysis	Observation COHSS reports attached to practical reports

Range of application
Practical investigations
COHSS reports.

013	Use specified text book to obtain specified information	Information needed to answer assignment

014	Manage own time	Receipt of set work

Range of application
Deadline for assignment
Deadline for practical reports.

BRIEF DESCRIPTION FOR MODULE CATALOGUE

This module introduced the principles of Biochemistry through a study of the structure and the role of biological macromolecules. Aspects covered include protein synthesis, protein structure-function relationships, carbon fixation and an overview of metabolism and the role of enzymes.

LEARNING/TEACHING METHODS

Lectures, group tutorial, based on pre-set work, assignments, computer simulation packages, practical work.

STUDENT DIRECTED LEARNING TIME

75 hours

CONTACT TIME

75 hours

ASSESSMENT COMPONENTS AND WEIGHTINGS

To successfully complete the module a minimum pass is required in each assessment component. Where the component is graded this will be D5, where the component is pass/fail a pass is required. The final module grade will be calculated from the graded assignment components in the proportions stated.

Test 1	Outcomes 01,02	25%
Test 2	Outcomes 01,02,05,06,09	25%
Practical Work	Outcomes 07,08,010,011,012,014	25%
Assignment	Outcomes 03,04,013,014	25%

A minimum attainment of D5 must be obtained in each component.

SCHEDULE OF ASSESSMENTS

Test 1	Module Week 5
Test 2	Module Week 15
Assignment	Out Module Week In Module Week 10

SITE   Main site

TIMETABLING   Semester 2

Indicative reading/learning resource

Any introductory biochemistry text, eg:
Stryer, *Biochemistry*, Freeman
Campbell, *Biochemistry*, Saunders College & Publishing
Smith & Wood, *Biological Molecules*, Chapman & Hall.

Chapter 14

Promoting Communication between Students and Staff in Large Subject-based Modular Programmes

Hugh Wilkins

Introduction

As demands on educators and educational establishments increase both in load and complexity, it becomes apparent that a key problem of many commercial organizations is also a problem in education. This problem – a lack of internal communication – may, in addition, be an enhanced characteristic of modular courses or vocational courses. The advantages of modular courses (flexibility, choice, individual selection) are well documented and very apparent; the disadvantages, however, are less clearly identified. A major disadvantage is the lack of communication between staff associated with individual and independent module areas. Programmes which combine a vocational area with modularity face a significant challenge in maintaining or developing an adequate level of internal communication. Courses which are both modular and vocational suffer, if that is the right word, from the need to employ staff with professional expertise over a wide range of disciplines. This results in a need for an explicit approach to communication as otherwise problems will arise with staff from diverse areas not understanding the subject areas and professional/industrial concerns and the module content of colleagues.

The problem: internal communications between staff

On our undergraduate degree programmes in hotel and catering management we at Oxford Brookes have a student population of about 400, undertaking a selection of modules from the basket of about 30 modules taught within the school. These modules cover a number of subject areas, including human resource management, economics, marketing, financial and strategic management, as well as the more closely identified vocational areas of accommodation management, food and beverage management, and operation management. The school employs a range of subject specialists including accountants, economists, marketeers and human resource managers, the majority of whom also have professional experience in the hotel and catering industry, as well as specialists in food and beverage and accommodation management. While staff are very competent and knowledgeable in the areas in which they are professionally focused, there is almost bound to be a limited understanding of other subject areas. Most staff will have a broad understanding of areas outside their specialism, but are comparatively unlikely to be fully aware of current issues.

Colleagues within a subject area experience a high degree of commonality in the delivery and assessment methods arising from teaching and the sharing of experiences. They frequently not only know the subject content of modules run by other staff, but also often understand the module objectives beyond the content, as defined in the syllabus. Colleagues from outside the specialist field, however, are almost bound to have a significantly lower awareness of the objectives and implementation methods beyond the (all too frequently bland) description contained in the syllabus.

This problem is compounded by some of the characteristics of higher education in that it is a *producer-led* process. Subject specialists may determine content in such a fashion that it is clearly understandable to colleagues within that subject area, but it may be less clear to the rest of the staff. As a result, there is a tendency for module descriptions to contain little explicit information and to rely heavily on implied detail. This problem is intensified when we start to address the skill development in modules, both of module-specific skills and of core or general skills.

Most modular systems use the concept of a personal tutor to help advise the student on the modules they should undertake. Staff are expected to be in a position to advise on all aspects of the modular course, helping the student to develop a comprehensive and focused programme, but without enhanced communication of module detail. This can be resolved by moving the module descriptions into a more explicit framework; more specifically, by developing outcome-focused module descriptions.

The solution: more explicit module descriptions

In addressing this problem area, Oxford Brookes University and the school of hotel and catering management have developed a process designed to help resolve the problems outlined above.

Few staff would question the assumption that each module develops knowledge, understanding and skills through the learning experience which students undertake. While a general understanding of the knowledge, understanding and professional or technical skills which are developed within a module is normal, it is unlikely that staff outside the subject group will fully know and understand the teaching/learning process which is undertaken. In consequence, they do not have a substantive clarity either of which, or how, the core or general skills are developed. The total experience students receive should be clearly defined within the module description. At Oxford Brookes we have recently decreed that all module descriptions be stated under four headings:

- *knowledge and understanding* (frequently developed through a lecture programme);
- *academic, professional and technical skills,* or module-specific skills (frequently developed through specific course assignments and workshops);
- *common and general skills* (developed in several ways through assignments, through workshops and through the assessment process); and
- *student learning experience* (the methodology of how the student develops the other aspects).

However, although it is relatively simple to re-transcribe a module description into a revised format, it is considerably less easy to persuade staff to invest time, energy and resources in adapting modules to what some might consider to be the trend of the year. In the first place this change process is dependent on staff having moved beyond the product-focused position of defining a module by subject content into a stance which evaluates the outcomes as measured by the summative and formative assessment processes. At this stage some staff may increase their resistance to the change process resulting from the dawning recognition that student perceptions of the outcomes of a module may differ radically from staff perceptions of module input and value. Resulting from recognition that the change process may be reluctantly received or possibly resisted, the school of hotel and catering management, under the guidance of Clive Robertson who is responsible for teaching and learning methods in the school, devised a process to minimize the resistance to change.

We identified that a key resource was students, and for two reasons. First, they were the recipients of the skills and knowledge development and second, they were the people who, through the use of independent study modules, could provide focused research on skills. In addition to this key resource, we provided an environment for staff to discuss skill development. We therefore encouraged a series of independent study modules undertaken by students who would receive academic credit and, in parallel, organized a series of off-site 'away-days' for staff. To date, students have completed three independent study modules and staff have attended three away-days. These away-days are often partially reliant on the output from the student independent study modules and we sometimes ask students to attend the away-day to make a presentation on their findings.

The method: independent study modules

Three independent study modules have been undertaken related to this area of interest. In these modules students need not only to negotiate and define the expected outcomes, but also to agree the method of demonstrating these outcomes. As a result, it is comparatively easy to define the module starting point allowing these modules to build cumulatively.

The first investigation was undertaken by a group of three students who analysed the skills students perceived as being developed within individual modules. This module was undertaken prior to the university being funded under the Enterprise Initiative and there was, perhaps, a marginally different interpretation of skill areas than has resulted from the work undertaken through the Enterprise Initiative. This module, through the use of student questionnaires and structured interviews, evaluated the core skills development within the Stage II, advanced modules. The results were identified as a percentage figure for the possible skill development within the module and the results were contained in a report. A summary of the report together with the key results were fed into the first of the away-days for staff, allowing staff to be more objective and critically analytical of their modules.

Meanwhile the university's enterprise office had developed a provisional list of 'enterprise skills' for consideration by course teams. The intent was to revise this list through consultation and then require that all courses should be reviewed in terms of their delivery of these skills. This was part of a university-wide decision to ensure that students graduated with a 'profile of their enterprise skills' (see Chapter 16 in this volume by Jenkins, Scurry and Turner).

The second investigation was undertaken by a group of two students who were able, at this later stage, not only to build on the work undertaken within the first independent study module, but also to relate specifically the skills to those identified through the Enterprise Initiative. Through the use of computer-analysed questionnaires they were able to sample a significantly large group of students. The research analysed, module by module, the student perception of the extent to which each of the enterprise skills was practised, taught and assessed. This allowed a reasonably comprehensive evaluation of the extent to which core or general skill development existed and effectively highlighted the skill areas which were neglected. This research also highlighted the contrast which existed between the practising, teaching and assessment of each skill. It was intended that the student-based research be contrasted with the staff perception of the extent to which each skill was developed in a module, but regrettably there was a low participation rate of staff and this analysis had to be abandoned. This research was fed into the second of the staff away-days.

The third investigation was designed to move one stage further and to correlate the staff perceptions of skill development in individual modules gained as a result of the second away-day, and students' perceptions of skill development. The intention of this independent study module, undertaken by an individual student, was to obtain a sample of draft profiles for graduating students. By necessity the intention was to sample only a small number of students and perhaps this project become over-focused on the staff perception of module content rather than the student perception. An area of complication for this student was that although there was a clear perception of what the content of a profile should be, there was less clarity over the format of the profile. A synthesis of the outcomes from this project were fed into the third away-day.

These student-led initiatives dovetail very effectively with the staff development programme which is also focused towards identifying, coordinating and communicating skill developments within modules. The concept of the away-day was developed from the need for staff to be away from the environment of the university and, therefore, to be free from conscious and subconscious interference with the process of concentrating on a specific task. The away-day is normally held at a nearby hotel or conference centre and will last the whole day. All staff are encouraged to attend.

The methods: away-days

The first away-day was designed to audit the level of skill development in modules as well as to raise, or create, staff awareness of outcomes-driven module formats. The away-day was successful in improving the awareness of the importance and level of skills development in modules as they are currently structured. The results of the first student independent study modules were an effective and important mechanism in developing a recognition amongst staff of the module content beyond that defined in the module guide. By the end of this workshop most module leaders had addressed the issue of what skills were being developed and assessed in their modules.

The second away-day was designed to build both on the first away-day and on the second student independent study module. It concluded the process of identifying our current position with the help of the second independent study module which had identified and evaluated the skill development in modules. It also allowed the process to be moved into the next stage, where a format for redefined module descriptions was adopted which was more explicit in defining the module content. This format was the one detailed earlier in this chapter.

The third away-day was intended to relate individual module outcomes to the overall degree objective in terms of all of the areas, ie knowledge and understanding, professional and technical skills, and general skills. A key input into this process was to be the third independent study module. By the end of this day it was intended that there would be some, albeit retrospectively, profiled students. In practice this final stage of the process was less successful than hoped as the move into producing profiled students was a more substantial leap than was realized.

At the end of this process nearly all modules within the school of hotel and catering management have been written in an explicit and outcomes-driven format enabling colleagues and students to have a clear understanding of the module content and its method of delivery and assessment. This will enable staff to advise students and will help students to choose modules, not only on the basis of the academic subject content, but also on the basis of which skills they wish to focus on in order to develop most effectively as individuals.

Conclusion

Reviewing the process, we are convinced that the mode of using independent study by students together with staff away-days is, in principle, an exceptionally effective method of implementing change. In our opinion the amount and rate of change would not have been achieved without this, or a similar, process. While it has by no means been fully effective, the vast majority of staff have embraced the changes enthusiastically. The away-days are effective in motivating, focusing and energizing staff to adopt and achieve change while the student input allows the process to be achieved faster and more effectively. As the pressure on staff, in most educational establishments, continues to increase, staff often become unable, or unwilling, to invest substantial amounts of time and energy in new ideas without the support which a process such as this can provide.

Chapter 15

The Use of Learning Contracts in Undergraduate Modular Programmes

Mike Laycock

For many higher education institutions the creation of a modular structure has presented both opportunities and challenges in offering students much more choice and flexibility in course provision. In the early stages of modularization the pattern of development seems to indicate a 'unitizing' of established courses with few opportunities for flexible learning (aside from 'optional' units). The change experienced, initially, is relatively minimal. In some ways this is understandable. Particular concerns of staff appear to centre on the dangers of establishing a fragmented learning framework in the creation of more flexibility. Among the issues for institutions which have pursued the modular route is the extent to which, in recognizing the development of cohort diversity, there can be an identifiable outcome integrity. For staff there are real concerns about learning development, progression and most important of all, coherence.

To manage progression and coherence many universities, such as the University of East London (UEL), which undertook a process of full modularization and semesterization for commencement in 1993/4, have implemented a system of 'co-requisites' and 'prerequisites'. Co-requisites and prerequisites are units which supply the body of knowledge and skills to fulfil the aims and objectives of complementary or subsequent units. Progression and coherence (or modular integration) are institutionally determined and prescribed, though student choice is enhanced through optional and elective units and single and combined honours degrees.

I have argued elsewhere (Laycock and Stephenson, 1993) that through the use of learning contracts it would be possible for an institution to provide a systematic framework based on the negotiation of learning, and thereby meet the needs and aspirations of students, rather than one which is wholly institutionally determined and with limited student choice. The framework is based on a more democratic partnership between the student, the institution and, where appropriate, employers, a partnership that would enhance student motivation and ownership of their studies. The framework would also provide procedures and mechanisms which recognize the backgrounds of a diverse student population. The recent McFarlane Report (1992) published by a working party of the Committee of Scottish Principals acknowledges deficiencies in the current system to take account of cohort diversity:

Substantial inefficiency within the current system is caused by a failure to take sufficient account of substantial differences in the readiness of entrants to study effectively within first-year courses ... . Besides the level of prior knowledge, it is also important to check on the extent to which entrants have effective study skills. At present, there seems to be a reluctance on the part of universities to take full account of this potential barrier to academic progress. (pp. 19–20)

The working party acknowledged the changes in higher education institutes (HEIs) sponsored by the Enterprise in Higher Education (EHE) initiative and the use of techniques associated with active and flexible learning promoting a

shift from formal, whole-class didactic teaching towards individual or group management of learning through the provision ... of structured resource materials, together with opportunities for the negotiation of tasks (often through specific 'learning contracts' drawn up to formalise requirements for the individual), self and peer-assessment, and collaborative work, often on real life projects. (McFarlane, 1992, p.5)

The University of East London's Enterprise Programme specifically sponsors, and has as its main aim, the use of learning contracts as a means by which students as individuals and members of learning groups can become responsible and accountable for their own learning and play an active part in planning, monitoring and providing evidence of achievement of that learning. The university's strategic plan offers glimpses of what may be built into modular development for the future. One of its priorities is to develop:

within the University's modularisation framework clear general entry requirements, flexible learning pathways and identifiable learning outcomes, as well as developing a consistent approach to the assessment of prior experimental learning *and offering each student guidance in creating individual learning plans.* (emphasis added)

The implication here is the importance of learning plans/contracts, in the diagnosis of previous knowledge, skills and experience and in planning to address 'readiness' to undertake their programme.

To avoid the problems identified, learning contracts might provide the basis for a systematic framework which will permit:

• the recognition of the backgrounds of a diverse student population;
• a means by which students can actively engage in planning and monitoring their own progress, and a means by which they can review and record their own learning;
• the development of a coherent study programme, which is created in the form of a partnership between the student, the institution and employers/

practitioners and which acknowledges the importance of the development of subject knowledge and its application, skill/competence, personal and professional development.

A 'wrap-around', planning, profiling and review framework

This chapter proposes the development of a modular unit that could be universally applicable to undergraduate modular programmes in HE. The framework is presented here in model form only – it has no basis in reality at undergraduate level though, at UEL, a modular unit, upon which this model is based, has been developed for the modular masters programme. At its heart is the use of a *learning contract/plan*. The educational basis of the framework would be process-oriented, rather than content-driven, permitting, simultaneously, a means by which students can plan, monitor and review their learning within a particular pathway and can address skills (study/transferable/professional) development deemed appropriate to the pathway.

The use of the term 'framework' is deliberate for the institutional mechanism by which the 'wrap' is delivered is highly dependent upon the structure and culture of individual institutions. The model could have a modular unit as its organizational basis but could also rely on a tutorial system for its delivery. Identifying the traditional role of the personal tutor is unhelpful in the context of the idea of a tutorial system since it implies a one-to-one relationship with students that would be impossible to resource. The model here would imply large group tutorials supported by staff with specialist expertise in facilitation.

The framework would have three distinct phases.

1. A *planning phase* during which students would:
   - review and reflect on prior learning. In some cases, students might stake claims for the assessment and accreditation of prior or prior experiential learning (AP(E)L). All students might be invited to audit current weaknesses in knowledge, skills and experience, addressing in particular weaknesses in study and other transferable skills;
   - justify the selection of units (where there is sufficient scope for choice through electives or options) for study and develop a *learning contract/ plan* which identifies learning goals, progression and development.
2. A *profiling and skills development phase* in which, while students pursue their selected units, they monitor their progress towards the attainment of unit learning outcomes. They also develop proficiency in study skills and personal transferable skills through a *core skills programme* and profile of their learning. Essentially students create, reflect upon and analyse their progression.
3. A *synoptic review or appraisal phase*. Though students would complete all required assessment they would also, for this unit, be required to submit a review or synoptic appraisal which might take the form of a *portfolio and critical review* of learning outcomes and progress achieved. For those

students who are considering leaving the university at any level but essentially for Level 3, the portfolio would act as a *record of achievement*. In diagrammatic form the three phases provide a 'wrap-around' integrative unit for any specialist pathway (see Figure 15.1) and can be produced, iteratively, for Levels 1, 2 and 3.

Planning phase and construction of the learning contract/plan

The first phase would build upon advisory tutorials to provide an intensive period of planning and diagnosis/self-diagnosis. Students would be expected to become familiar with the available content modules but would also be expected to:
- review previous strengths and weaknesses in knowledge, skills and experience;
- engage in a self-diagnosis of study and personal transferable skills;
- examine the coherence of their modular pathway.

Staff would introduce the units of relevance to the particular pathway together with possibilities for choices or options, the facilities for learner support, the ways in which students might develop personal transferable skills and an introduction to the learning outcomes defined for each unit.

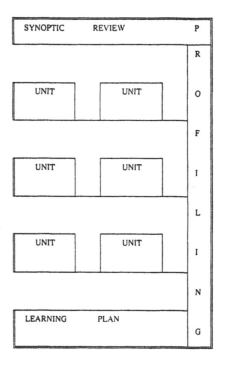

Figure 15.1 *A model framework*

This first phase would conclude with the submission of a learning contract/ plan for formative assessment. (See Figure 15.2).

STAFF

Introduction to units choices/ options	Introduction to learner support	Introduction to personal transferable skills units	Introduction to learning outcomes of

STUDENTS

Review of previous knowledge/ skills/ experience	Diagnosis of study/personal transferable skills	Establish personal/ career development plan	Learning Contract/ plan 1. Formulate proposed and coherent programme of study. 2. Anticipate likely requirements in terms of study/ personal transferable skills 3. Personal criteria for self-appraisal. 4. Appreciate learning outcomes for self and those expected by staff.

Figure 15.2 *Planning phase*

Monitoring and skills development phase

During the second phase, when students are fully engaged with their specialist content units, the unit would complement specialist work by requiring students to articulate their approach to pathway studies, to monitor and record their own progress and to provide periodic action plans.

The main contents, however, might involve the development of core personal transferable skills development (not otherwise covered by other pathway units) that is planned and progressive through levels of study.

Core skills development

A programme of core personal transferable skills development within, for example, project work, during this phase would be accredited, with students providing the necessary evidence of having met learning outcomes documented in their portfolio. Assessment might be by both peer and tutor. It is recognized that the majority of personal transferable skills will be integral to the development of pathways and may be integrated within content units. However, individual pathways can establish which core skills, not covered by content units, could be included in this phase.

Synoptic review or appraisal phase

The process would conclude with the submission of a portfolio in which students document evidence of skills development and of having profiled progress in their studies for the particular level.

It would involve assessing the extent to which they feel their own learning outcomes have been achieved and those for other units. Evidence of achievement, together with documentation of core skills development and assessment, would be presented in the portfolio of achievement. This would be accompanied by a synoptic appraisal of learning progression by a critical review of all work undertaken at that level. The portfolio is essentially descriptive and the critical review evaluative. At the point of exit from the university students would edit all portfolio work and the result be included in a final, summative record of achievement.

Functions of the framework

Fundamentally the framework would emphasize the importance of critical reflection and review and the planned, progressive development of core skills. By repeating the unit iteratively, students can develop increasing levels of sophistication in skills development as they progress to greater knowledge acquisition and a greater complexity of situations in which to demonstrate these.

While the framework would also enhance coherence and progression within a modular scheme, a number of other important functions are fulfilled. The framework:

- acknowledges the diverse nature of the student intake and enables the diagnosis of need in relation to learner support;
- encourages students to take responsibility (and to be accountable) for their own learning;
- encourages ownership of study;
- permits an active engagement with student progress and student feedback;
- it provides a consistent, individual level or 'entry to exit' home-base for students.

Resource-based/open learning

Current ideas about the future of higher education suggest that traditional organizational structures and forms of educational provision are giving way to a scenario where students enter and exit tailored programmes, using a mix of multi-media resource-material-based learning.

The many current initiatives attempting to promote what is generally termed resource-based learning often include the important learning process issues in open learning of learner-managed learning (using a variety of techniques and devices such as learning contracts/plans, profiling, portfolio development etc). It is vital that resource-based approaches do not represent yet another form of passive learning with students simply directed to watch videos, sit in front of PCs, listen to audio tapes or read printed materials, with few opportunities for critical dialogue (even though computer-based learning software may be 'interactive' [CBL]) between peers and tutors. For students, there are dangers of highly individuated and alienating learning experiences; and for staff, the feeling that their 'teaching' skills are devalued or worse, unnecessary.

In the progressive move in higher education towards open and flexible learning, with more and more course content converted to packaged instruction, the need for a 'wrap-around' framework may become ever more apparent. It would provide the contextual home in which students and staff can jointly plan the coverage of content, monitor progression and understanding and engage in critical dialogue about all that has been seen, read or heard by the student. It would become the means to secure quality feedback and interactivity.

In summary, the framework would draw together many of the current ideas and techniques designed to support student responsibility in learning and to encourage the development of the lifelong learner.

Delivery of the framework

For most institutions, the addition of specific modular units through which the phases outlined can be delivered and credit awarded will require a reappraisal of the current credit awarded to content units within any one modular pathway. If operated on a level (or 120 credits) basis, credit awarded for the unit would inevitable mean credit lost to a content unit. At UEL one unit attracts 20 credits and thus, if the framework were delivered as a unit or a half unit, either 20 or 10 credits would be removed from a subject content unit or units. Using a compulsory or universal unit would conceivably meet with institutional opposition. Modularization and semesterization have, however, already required staff to reconsider the syllabus and 'essential' subject coverage given concerns about overall validity and/or professional requirements. Being operated as an elective or optional unit would perhaps be more acceptable, though students who might benefit from the process may not avail themselves of it. Ultimately, individual institutions must decide how it can be resourced and, if credit should be awarded, if the process itself is recognized as an important contribution to their educational provision. Different variants of the framework could, of course, exist within an institution. If the process were delivered through a unit, an institution would, in effect, be signifying that lifelong learning starts from a process of actively engaging learners in solving the problem of their own higher education and reflections on solutions to it. Institutional priorities and purposes would be reflected in the structure of provision.

Many of the current teaching and learning techniques, invariably operating as discrete elements of some programme areas, could coalesce to become the focal point for the development of the learner's confidence, competence and capability.

This model unit has been developed from the work already undertaken by the team devising the modular masters programme at the University of East London. I am particularly indebted to the work of John Cocking and Jim Graham. It is also part of on-going developmental work with Professor John Stephenson (director, Higher Education for Capability).

References

McFarlane Report (1992) *Teaching and Learning in an Expanding Higher Education System*, report of a working party of the committee of Scottish Principals, Polton House Press.

Laycock, M and Stephenson, J (1993) *Using Learning Contracts in Higher Education*, London: Kogan Page.

Chapter 16

Using Profiling to Integrate Skill Development in a Large Modular Course

Alan Jenkins, David Scurry and David Turner

The modular structure makes it difficult, but not impossible to ensure the systematic development of interpersonal and communication skills. HMI Report on Oxford Polytechnic (DES, 1991, p 8)

In higher education... the term profiling is being used to describe the ... processes of empowering students to be involved in the assessment, recording and reviewing of their own personal development and learning. ... The formative process, is then, at the heart of development, but many would see the production of an end document or summative record as equally important to students, employers and other 'end users' of such documents in that they provide a more rounded picture of an individual than a narrow list of examination results. (Assiter and Shaw, 1993, p. 20)

Our story is one of a large well-established modular course in transition. It is an account of one institution's attempt to integrate profiling and a coherent programme for students' skills development within a large complex modular course. Two of us, David Scurry as dean and David Turner as assistant dean, have responsibility for the academic development and administrative management of the course; Alan Jenkins works in the Enterprise Unit, which is developing an institutional policy to profile all students.

First we outline the main features of the modular course at Oxford Brookes and consider its successes and failures in developing students' capabilities and transferable skills. We then outline the central features of profiling and explain why it is an effective way of developing students' skills. We then turn to our central theme – what we have achieved so far and what has yet to be resolved in our attempts to integrate the profiling of student skills into a large modular course.

The modular course at Oxford Brookes

The modular course at Oxford Brookes (formerly Oxford Polytechnic) began in 1972 in selected science subjects. It has since extended across most (and perhaps soon all) of the institution and in September 1993 there were nearly 6,000 students enrolled in some 90 subjects or 'fields' of study (eg, art history, physics, etc. Detailed features of the scheme are set out in Watson *et al.*, 1989). Its central features are:

- it is a credit accumulation scheme. Most students choose three fields (subjects) in Year 1 and two fields or subjects in the advanced Stage 2. There is no distinction between Year 2 and Year 3 modules;
- individual subject groups have considerable autonomy within centrally determined rules and values;
- there are three terms per academic year;
- full-time students will generally take three or four separate courses or modules each term, most of which will be assessed in that term;
- students receive a broad subject-based education;
- students have to complete the minimum requirements in order to take advantage of the available choices;
- students are active participants in designing their own programmes of study. In Year 1 they are required to choose modules outside their chosen fields (subject specialisms); in Stage 2, there is generally considerable choice within their two fields and, to an extent, outside them;
- as most modules last only one term and are assessed in that term, students get a termly transcript recording their progress and aspects of their performance.

This has been a highly successful course and one that has been adapted by many institutions within the UK. It has demonstrated two great strengths. First, it has encouraged different subject groups to develop teaching and assessment methods appropriate to their disciplines, while ensuring effective central administration and academic development for the course as a whole. Second, it has proved flexible and has been able to accommodate new developments in higher education. Part-time education, the Diploma in Higher Education, professionally-based courses such as health care studies, accelerated degrees – all have been readily integrated into its developing structure. Each has helped invigorate the course by forcing it to reassess its practice and values.

Many successes with some shortcomings

Alongside its other successes, the modular course has proved effective in developing student skills and capabilities. The autonomy of the subject groups has enabled many of them to develop innovative and successful ways of integrating subject-specific and general skills into their courses (see for example the accounts of English, geography, and hotel and catering management in this book). Students see that the modular structure of the course empowers them and helps them to develop certain skills, particularly in managing their time and tasks (see the students' comments in the Introduction).

However, as these comments also indicate, there are limitations and shortcomings. An inspection of the modular course by Her Majesty's Inspectors in October and November 1990 reported (DES, 1991):

The modular structure makes it difficult, but not impossible, to ensure the systematic development of interpersonal and communication skills. Some fields have an agenda for the development of such skills through planned activities linked to clear objectives and with opportunities for feedback to students. In most fields, however, tutors view the development of these skills simply in terms of increasing the levels of student participation in classes. *The example of good practice remains isolated.* (p.8, emphasis added)

The academic aims of some fields are less well articulated, making it difficult to develop systematically the appropriate range of subject specific and learning skills. (p.15)

On entry, students are assigned a personal tutor ... . In principle, the personal tutor plays a key role within the modular course. For the majority of students who study two single fields he/she is the one person who has oversight of a student's whole programme. However, personal tutors can have up to 24 students at a given time and receive no timetable relief to carry out their responsibilities. Responses from some students suggest that personal tutors are approachable and supportive, but, generally, react to problems which are identified, rather than taking the initiative in providing academic guidance. (p. 11)

In their conclusion they recommended that one of

the specific issues which might be further addressed .... (was) *the systematic development of subject specific, interpersonal and communication skills within each field.* (p. 17, added emphasis)

An Enterprise programme

Oxford Brookes' successful bid to the Department of Employment's Enterprise Fund was in part aimed at helping the institution tackle these problems. Specifically we committed ourselves to:

- ensuring that all students graduate with a profile of their enterprise skills and qualities;
- reviewing all our courses in terms of their delivery of enterprise skills.

A provisional list of enterprise skills (communication, problem-solving etc) demonstrated our commitment as an institution to a skills-based curriculum. This was an ambitious commitment. Most of the other 'Enterprise' institutions had committed themselves to specific initiatives in limited areas. Ours was an institutional commitment and one which would involve significant changes to the structure and practices of the modular course.

Profiling and recording achievement

Profiling developed first in schools and is now being taken up by many HEI in the UK. Though there is no one model or definition, we see its central features as:

- clear specification – in a language that is clear to students – of what learning is expected or required of them by the end of a course;
- methods of teaching and assessment that are chosen and monitored to ensure that students can learn what is expected or required;
- structured conversations between students and tutors (and between students) which enable students to record what they already know, to understand better what is expected of them, and to plan their own learning;
- students being encouraged or required systematically to collect evidence of their developing knowledge and achievement;
- well organized administrative support for students and tutors in this process.

We consider it useful to distinguish between profiling – a formative *process* which puts students at the centre of planning and monitoring their learning – and a final *record* of achievement which records their profile as a learner at the end of this degree course. This final record should be useful to the learner but also to potential employers, giving a clearer and fuller description of the student than the usual academic transcript.

Profiling the advantages to both students and staff some of these are set out below:

Advantages to students
- clear statements of required learning and criteria for assessment;
- clear information about progress;
- a recording of skills and abilities;
- structured gathering of evidence of skills;
- diagnostic conversations with staff;
- action planning for the future;
- a record of achievement for employers;
- greater responsibility for own learning and control over self-presentation.

Advantages to staff
- clear statements of required learning and criteria for assessment;
- individual maps of students' progress;
- a common language for discussing skills and abilities;
- better information for counselling students;
- opportunity to promote students to potential employers;
- systems of assessment which are relevant and accountable.

When an institution or large modular course commits itself to profiling and records of achievement, it is committing itself to significant changes to its teaching and assessment practices and recording systems. It is also committing itself to becoming an institution which systematically develops the skills and capabilities of its students. In a large modular course this involves major cultural and administrative changes.

(Partial) solutions to the problems of integrating profiling into the modular course

At the time of writing (March 1994) many policy decisions have been made and in some areas the impact is already being felt as policy decisions are implemented in the practices of teaching and learning. In other areas, policy has yet to be resolved and in many areas the practice of profiling has yet to start.

At first the meaning, values and principles of profiling were a foreign language to most staff and students. There were few examples of practice within the institution to use as models, with the professional areas of nursing and education as the major exceptions. Initially we explained profiling through workshops and working documents; we also funded subject groups that wanted to take the lead in profiling and developing a skills-based curriculum (see for example the account of hotel and catering management in Chapter 14 in this volume).

We sought to extend and deepen the 'isolated ... examples of good practice' that the HMIs had noted. The institution had much good practice to build upon; the recently added health care fields had been designed with carefully defined competences and negotiated learning contracts. However, in extending the philosophy of recognizing and accrediting students' capabilities and skills to all fields we met much resistance and considerable organizational difficulties. The resistance came largely from two groups of staff: from those wedded to a subject-specific curriculum in which the teacher traditionally dominates; and those who rejected a 'Thatcherite' emphasis on employability skills. We have in part sought to meet these fears by emphasizing that our approach to a 'capability curriculum' is one that is delivered through the methods used in teaching and assessing the traditional subjects.

As part of the programme to implement the systematic profiling of skills across the institution, subject groups, when they come up for a major review, are required to describe their modules to a revised format. This ensures students, colleagues and institutional review committees identify their stated practice in these areas. We recognize this is only a start; as Chapter 14 by Hugh Wilkins indicates, what is then written on paper is not necessarily what immediately becomes practice. But it is a start – and sometimes policy has to lead hearts and minds. Moreover we have noticed a significant change in the attitude of staff to skills as they develop their own confidence and particular practices in integrating skills and profiling to the concerns of their discipline.

Transferable and core skills

Like many other institutions, we started to define the transferable skills the course might deliver through considering the lists of skills developed through BTEC and employers groups in the UK, North America and elsewhere. To an extent these had shaped the provisional list of skills in our Enterprise bid. We eventually decided that the way forward – the way which would gather most staff support and be more compatible with the modular course – was to start by studying the skills that were either implicitly or explicitly developed in subjects as they were now taught. From these we developed a list of five broad categories of skills. These are:

- *self management* – the ability of students to manage their own learning development;
- *learning skills* – the ability of students to learn effectively and be aware of their own learning strategies;
- *communication* – the ability of students to express ideas and opinions with confidence and clarity to a variety of audiences for a variety of purposes;
- *teamwork* - the ability of students to work productively in different kinds of teams;
- *problem-solving* – the ability of students to identify the main features of a given problem and develop strategies for its resolution.

In February 1994 the university agreed to this list of skills and decreed that all courses/fields should be required to 'deliver' (unless it could give good reasons) all these skills as an integral (or separate) part of the way their subject was taught.

The issue of whether there were certain 'core' transferable skills presented fundamental problems to those of us (David Scurry, David Turner and others) responsible for its academic leadership and management of the modular course.

The key people in the move to deliver and profile skills in the curriculum were intrigued and excited by ideas of a core curriculum and core skills. Brian Roper, then pro-Vice Chancellor, Lawrie Walker, Enterprise Director, and Alan Jenkins, Profiling Coordinator, had visited institutions in North America, in particular the University of Denver and Alverno College. They were enthusiastic about Alverno's core curriculum of eight ability areas, the specification of these abilities at various levels, and the role of the disciplines as vehicles for delivering these abilities, and on their return discussed how to adapt these ideas to our culture and practice.

For some colleagues these were exciting ideas and a way of invigorating a modular course that for them had become too settled and concerned with administrative rules. Others saw it as an assault on university education and the development of a low-level skills education or as an attack on what was particularly valuable – in Rob Pope's phrase in Chapter 7 in this volume, the 'peculiar practices' of the different disciplinary ways of knowing.

We feared that the ideas of core curriculum and core skills were incompatible with the traditions of our modular course. The culture and the ideology of the modular course emphasizes choice and considerable autonomy for the subject groups. Modules are defined at only two levels, basic and advanced. Though subject groups do in part restrict choice and ensure progression through recommendations and compulsory modules, the overall pattern of the modular degree is a number of compulsory modules for each field in Stage 1 and then considerable choice and flexibility in Stage 2.

If skills were to be defined at three or four levels, this could conflict with the way that academic fields were structured. It might also affect the options available to students. If, for example, modules in Egyptology that also delivered advanced problem-solving could only be taken by students who had taken modules in Egyptology that had delivered introductory problem solving, student choice would be further reduced. We also feared that students might have to develop – wastefully – the same skills in both their fields. As the proposals were developed, our fears abated and we now see skills profiling as a way of invigorating the course, developing students' abilities and being entirely compatible with the modular philosophy.

Students at Oxford Brookes will soon have a modular course that guarantees them a fuller, richer, though more complicated range of choices. Already our modular handbook (which informs students of their choice of modules) lists 'G' by some of our modules. This G indicates 'there is normally group work involved in the assessment of these modules' (Oxford Brookes University, 1993, p.91). The handbook will soon list the five skills areas with their linked modules. As fields produce 'skills maps' showing where these skills are taught, practised and assessed, students will be able to make a more complex but 'richer' set of choices to develop their own particular programme. The fact that two fields may develop the same or similar skills is perhaps less of a problem than we first thought. We expect that different subject groups will develop these skills in particular ways reflecting their own discipline and practices. Furthermore, as long as students are clearly informed of what to expect – through effective handbooks and the like – it is their choice as to whether to repeat particular skills. In addition to the current transcript recording the modules taken and grades received, we expect students shortly to receive a transcript recording the 'transferable' skills they have practised. This will be part of a final record of achievement and, we hope, useful both to the student and to potential employers. It is possible that as these new practices are incorporated in the course, we will return to the question of how to specify skills at various levels and to ensure their coherent development.

Profiling different skills

In developing profiling as an intrinsic part of the modular course we have distinguished between three distinct areas for profiling: field-based, personal profiling, and a record of achievement.

- *field- (course-) based profiling* is the process of reflection, recording and forward planning in relation to the learning that occurs within an identified course or field of study;
- *personal profiling* is the process by which a student reflects upon and records his or her overall learning progress while at university. This

includes extracurricular achievements such as being a student representative, working in a community group or a local school as well as learning
achievements in his or her fields of study (see Chapter 12 in this volume).
The student can then use that self-knowledge to plan future life goals;
- *a record of achievement* is a summary record, prepared towards the end of a
  student's degree course, using evidence from the profiling process which
  identifies the skills, knowledge and achievements gained while at
  university.

As staff have come to see course-based profiling as a way of developing their
own approach to learning through the discipline, they have generally
become positive to these changes. Different subject groups have started to
experiment with ways of delivering profiling that reflect the particular way
their field is constructed. For example, the English field has a compulsory
module at the end of Stages 1 and 2 of their course. In these modules, each
student has been required to write a reflective essay on their learning in the
English field. Staff teaching courses or fields with very different structures,
who wish to include such reflective essays, will have to find alternative ways
of delivering course based profiling. There are now at least four ways of the
meeting university's requirements for course-based profiling. English
studies, geology, education and adult nursing have each developed a
distinct approach and we expect staff to develop further models. (The full
list of student entitlements to course-based and personal profiling are set out
in Chapter 2 in this volume).

At Brookes we believe that the structures and practices of the modular
course will facilitate the widespread adoption of profiling to develop student
capability. Modular courses offer significant advantages over discipline-
based departmental or faculty structures and cultures. At one level, strong
central regulations can require such developments and ensure students
certain common entitlements. More positively, our modular course brings
together staff from across the university in a wide range of committees and
encounters. Though disciplinary conflicts are sometimes played out in these
meetings, they also result in staff learning from each others' values and
practices. In meetings one now hears staff discussing alternative models of
delivering a skill-based curriculum and debating the effect of different
assessment systems on the development of student skills; so in this crucial
respect modular courses can lead to significant change across an institution
to a skill-based curriculum.

As we conclude this account, we report on a problem we have yet to
resolve. Readers will recall the HMI's comments on the inadequacies of our
personal tutor system; staff having 'up to 24 students at a given time and
[receiving] no timetable relief to carry out their responsibilities' (HMI, 1991,
p.11). Since that time student:staff ratios have increased as have the
pressures for staff to pursue research ratings and rankings. Much of the fear
and opposition of academic staff to profiling was the very real fear that
(personal) profiling would yet again increase their workload.

Our personal tutor system was established as the modular course began
and the role of the personal tutor was then seen as a central way of helping

the students orientate themselves to the course and reflect on where they were going. Then, personal tutors had time to get to know their tutees. Now it is largely a question of a hurried few minutes of form-filling per term and both staff and students complain of the inadequacies of the personal tutor system.

Short of the shift of resources to higher education, the institution will be faced with some harsh choices. These include the following:

- recognizing that the personal tutor system cannot be maintained in any form in British higher education, at least at Oxford Brookes. Though we see that personal profiling offers considerable benefits to developing student capability, it is a 'service' we cannot provide;
- requiring staff to work even harder, increasing their responsibilities and using the carrot and stick of rewards and appraisal to encourage them to perform. We expect they would capably resist this and destroy any chance of success for personal profiling;
- shifting resources from elsewhere – from research, from the taught curriculum, from central services – to resource a revised personal tutor system;
- revising the way the personal tutor system operates, moving to staff working with whole groups of personal tutees, and perhaps selected students being credited for helping in this process;
- crediting students and staff for the learning involved in personal profiling. One of the early proposals was to create what was then termed a 'long thin module' running through the degree programme. This is essentially the principle in Mike Laycock's discussion of a learning contract in Chapter 15 in this volume. In general, students strongly supported this idea; staff vociferously rejected the idea – they saw it taking resources away from academic studies. Though we expect some subject groups to develop such profiling modules, we know this idea must – for the moment – be put aside as a central institutional response. Other modular courses, particularly those that are just developing, may well decide to adopt the profiling module.

Conclusions

We have long worked in a modular course structure and the experience has convinced us that it is an efficient, cost-effective structure, and one that does empower students to make their own choices. In terms of capability skills we know it encourages – even requires - students to work consistently and manage their time and tasks. We also recognize that our modular course has emphasized staff views of the importance of subject-based knowledge and generally has neglected the systematic development of skills. Our experience so far is that profiling offers a way of integrating skill development across a large complex modular course.

We also recognize that at present, while we have largely solved the political and organizational problems, the practice of integrating these skills into how students learn has yet to pervade the course. Course-based profiling is a way of ensuring that a skills-based curriculum is an entitlement for all students. However, we also believe that without a shift and/or a reorganization of resources to a revitalized personal tutor system, this course-based profiling will be only a partial move to a skills-based curriculum.

Furthermore, a well developed personal profiling system would reaffirm one of the most important principles of modular courses – that students should be empowered to make effective choices. Higher student:staff ratios have effectively stripped bare the personal tutor system. Personal profiling offers a way of enabling students to consider systematically the choices they make in designing their course and to make an informed choice of the skills they wish to develop. Profiling is a central way of ensuring that a modular course supports the development of student capability.

References

Assiter, A and Shaw, E (1993) *Using Records of Achievement in Higher Education*, London: Kogan Page.

Department of Education and Science (1991) *The Modular Course at Oxford Polytechnic: A report by HMI*, Stanmore, Middlesex: DES.

Oxford Brookes University (1993) *Modular Course Prospectus 1993–94*, Oxford Brookes University.

Watson, D, Brooks, J, Coghill, C, Lindsay, R and Scurry, D (1989) *Managing the Modular Course: Perspectives from Oxford Polytechnic*, Buckingham: Society for Research with Higher Education and Open University Press.

SECTION E:
TOWARDS THE FUTURE

Chapter 17

Capability and the Future of Modularity: An Institutional Perspective

Brian Roper

Introduction

Modularity in Britain is now some 20 years old and my own institution (formerly as Oxford Polytechnic) was associated with modularity from the outset. Oxford Brookes University now has 11,000 students, 70 per cent of whom are following modular courses primarily at undergraduate level, where over 70 single and double fields of study are offered. Throughout this period, and more especially in the past five years, we have sought to resolve an apparent contradiction. The problem is how, within binding resource constraints, we should reconcile increasing student choice and empowerment *and* also ensure that students have the opportunity to develop their capability and skills.

In what follows I shall ground the debate in an understanding of the contemporary context of British higher education; stylize the current debate about the transition to a form of modularity better suited to graduate needs of the 21st century; mount a critique of our present approach to the learning offer; and offer a proposal for future development.

The context

Higher education in Britain has undergone a major transformation in the past 30 years yet certain fixed points remain. At the risk of gross over-simplification the salient features would appear to be the following:

- An increase in the size of the HE sector as measured by the increased numbers of degree awarding bodies (post the Education Reform Act) and by an increase in the number of home admissions to first-year full-time and sandwich degree courses of 93 per cent since 1987, exceeding 200,000 in 1992. In November 1993 the Department for Education announced that, for the first time, total enrolments had exceeded 1 million.
- An increase in the participation rate of 18-year old school leavers (from 11 per cent in 1987 to 28 per cent by 1992, and to around 30 per cent by November 1993 in England and Wales) and increases in both the number and proportion of 'non-standard entrants' resulting in an increase in the demand for places of over 25 per cent between 1987 and 1992.
- Changes in the ethnic and gender balances in the HE student population but with evidence of continuing élitism in terms of the narrowness of the social class entry to HE with 62 per cent of university entrants coming from social classes I and II.
- Slow recognition by HEIs of the implications of these patterns for their own practices.
- Continued hegemony of academic tribalism with the implicit objective of training the next generation of academics.
- The increasingly explicit pursuit of publishable and cited research upon which rests peer approval and advancement.
- The continuing dominance of producer-led curricula and assessment processes lying alongside demand-led structural innovation (part-time, mixed mode, CATS-rated provision).
- The increased pressure of public accountability in counterpoint to increased operating autonomy (through 'independence').
- The need to demonstrate the maintenance (at least) of the quality of provision in an era of unprecedented productivity increases and against a background of decreasing real state expenditure per student and increasing student indebtedness.
- The continuing mismatch between state-sponsored encouragement of study in certain areas and a deficiency of student demand for them (engineering, technology and physical sciences) as against a sustained excess demand for other areas which, at least implicitly, are thought to be less worthy of such support (business and administration, humanities and social sciences).
- An unclear relationship between the supply of graduates and labour market needs. According to the Institute of Manpower Studies the huge rise in graduate numbers has altered the labour market 'beyond recognition'; the dilution of the notion of 'graduate' jobs and 'graduate' employers; the appearance of sustained periods of structural and not

merely cyclical graduate unemployment; continuing employer preference for the graduates of 'old' universities (11 per cent unemployment of
graduates of old universities compared with 18 per cent for new
universities in the autumn of 1993).

- The emergence of market or near-market pressures upon universities
through state-sponsored drives for increased efficiency at a time of
limited opportunities to reduce dependence on state funding. While the
HEFCE recurrent grant is planned to increase from £3,096m in 1994/5 to
£3,342m in 1996/7 it is expected to ensure that pay increases are met by
'efficiency improvements'.
- Increasing price competition for certain HEI goods and services.
- The continual dominance of staffing as a proportion of total university
costs (approximately 70 per cent), but with little linkage between
individual performance and remuneration.
- The sector remaining, almost exclusively, characterized by not-for-profit
charitable organizations acting in competition for both students and staff
and in concert only in defence of a common foe, perennially state-
funding.
- A continued and increasingly apparent (through league-tabling and
inspection) hierarchy of providers.
- A sharp brake on institutions' expansionary intentions as confirmed in
the November 1993 budget statement.
- A continued drive for efficiency savings (currently of the order of 2–3 per
cent per annum and soon to rise to 4 per cent per annum) in recurrent
revenue through the HEFCE funding mechanisms. This adds to the real-
terms reduction in funding per student which has occurred since 1987.
- The real reduction in tuition fees for courses in humanities, social
sciences, business and related areas introduced in 1992 and the 45 per
cent across-the-board reduction in fees for all bands announced in the
November 1993 budget.
- Limited further external earnings opportunities, beyond the one-third of
universities' income currently derived from non-government sources,
due to the demand for short courses and consultancies being adversely
affected by the recession; the continuing difficulty faced by most
universities in generating genuinely 'free' endowment income; recruitment difficulties experienced in some international markets.
- Continuing limitations on publicly-funded capital for adaptations and
new building of teaching accommodation and a continuing difficulty of
generating private loan facilities for other than residential purposes. In
May 1993 the CVCP estimated the cost of clearing the teaching buildings
maintenance backlog alone to be £1.35bn.
- Continuing higher education cost increases above the general level in the
economy, estimated at 11 per cent more than the out-turn GDP since
1985/6 and this despite a deterioration in average student staff ratios from
11:1 in 1987/8 to 14:1 in 1991/2.
- Increasing student indebtedness due to the reduction of maintenance
grants, with the November 1993 budget statement announcing an

intention to bring maintenance grants and loans into balance by 1996/7, by progressive reduction of the former; the insufficient level of hardship funds; cost increases above the rate of inflation and limited term-time and vacation paid-work opportunities.

- The possible introduction of mechanisms designed to ensure that the maintenance and/or tuition fee costs of future expansion are increasingly borne by students and/or graduates (voucher systems, graduate taxation, employer payroll taxation, etc). It has been argued that such policies are necessary, on equity grounds, to reflect the positive private rate of return enjoyed by graduates in the labour market. It would appear that this view now enjoys CVCP and cross-party parliamentary support and is a central feature of the National Commission on Education's report, *Learning to Succeed* (Report of the Paul Hamlyn Foundation, 1993).
- Increased personal, family and peer group beliefs that higher education is an increasingly realistic expectation.
- An increase in the supply of places, particularly marked up to 1992.
- The improved formal entry qualifications of traditional applicants and the preparedness of most universities to evaluate seriously non-traditional entrants' ability to benefit by reference to other criteria.
- The lagged effects of both the government's redirection of student number growth to the further education sector (which is due to expand by 25 per cent over the next three years) and the increased staying-on rate in schools (from 50 per cent in the mid-1980s to over 70 per cent in 1993).
- The projection of larger 18-year old cohorts in the population post-1996 and the continuing growth in demand from non-standard entrants. This projected growth adds to the 80 per cent increase in student numbers experienced since 1979.
- A more explicit, but still to be formalized, hierarchy of providers based on their research prowess much buttressed by the recent UFC Research Assessment Exercise and the allocation decisions of the Research Councils which accentuate selectivity.
- A consequential and currently conflicting set of processes through which some universities seek to improve their positioning in the research domain thereby threatening 'mission drift'. This may be held to threaten pre-degree provision and the widening of participation in higher education.
- Increasing pressure from near-university institutions ('university colleges' and major metropolitan FE colleges seeking polytechnic status) inducing some universities to re-evaluate their position.
- The attempt by some universities to identify and market distinctive characteristics, which niches they might occupy based on 'product' or other differentiation, eg curricular offering, cost or locational advantage. It should be noted that there are developing cost-derived pressures for students to study at their neighbourhood university. Further, it should be noted that Mark 1 modular course provision at undergraduate level is now very widespread and not restricted to new universities.

- An increasingly better informed (through public league tables) and demanding clientele (through charter style developments and the exercise of choice).

The implications of this assessment are: that exchequer-funded resourcing will continue to deteriorate and that income diversification and cost containment will become increasingly prominent features; that the momentum towards mass higher education in Britain and the move towards a more diverse student intake is now capable only of being slowed and not of being stopped; that increased consumer (student) choice coupled with major structural adjustments in the supply of higher education are likely to become more pronounced with the learning offer becoming the issue of greatest interest and scrutiny.

The Issue

Major changes to the nature of the undergraduate learning offer have become apparent in British higher education. Modularization is rampant and semesterization is incipient. These are structural responses to improving the learning offer but their predication requires further analysis. A necessary starting point is to consider the dominant culture of higher education. Some of the salient features could be argued to be that:

- Staff (by which is usually meant teaching staff) welfare is frequently held to be synonymous with student welfare, there may even be thought to be a direct causality.
- Students are not the real clients; they are but one of a multiplicity of stakeholders.
- The (subject) producer knows best or all; this is supply-side education.
- Even if the third point is not valid, the students either do not know what they want or, if they do, do not know how to judge what is in their own best interests. This proposition is then inescapably linked to the previous proposition.

The general culture described above takes a particular form in discussion of modular course structures. Modularization in the UK is now some 20 years old and has been the subject of widespread adoption, particularly, but not exclusively, in the ex-polytechnic sector. While the precise arrangements differ, Mark I modular courses have the following characteristics:

- The delivery structures and the all-important rules matter a very great deal, almost to the exclusion of the overall aims and philosophy.
- The appearance, and not necessarily the reality, of 'choice' and 'flexibility' matters more than 'coherence' and 'progression'.
- Apparent 'choice' and 'flexibility' are confused with real student 'entitlement' and 'empowerment'.
- Limited though real 'choice' and 'flexibility' may be bought at great resource and logistical cost.
- Extensive multi-disciplinarity but limited inter-disciplinarity is evident save in project work.

- In seeking to join the Mark I modular club or in seeking to progress to a higher stage of development – which we might call Mark II modularity – universities have, for the reasons given above, a daunting task. Progress is unlikely to be easy. My experience suggests that those who would engage in curricular change on this scale are likely to be met with the following killer phrases and other anti-coagulants:

> 'We haven't got the staff'.
> 'It's all right in theory but can you put it into practice?'.
> 'You don't understand the problem (it's all right for you but …)'.
> 'We have too much to do already'.
> 'Let's set up a committee'.
> 'You'll never get management and/or the staff to agree to that'.
> 'It's too late' (a variation of 'it's too soon').
> 'We're doing it already'.
> 'It's not our responsibility'.
> 'They've already tried it in the USA (Australia, Canada, University X, etc) and have abandoned it'.
> 'Vision is a dangerous thing (so too are planning and a determination to achieve)'.
> 'The Enterprise project will do it (all) for us'.

The progression to Mark II modularity dictates a reconsideration of the underlying rationale for higher education. It requires universities to be outward looking, to be centred upon the wider development of students and their experience as learners, employees and citizens and to be at least as serious in this pursuit as they have historically been in the disciplinary and research domains.

The present approach: the instructional curriculum

Conventionally, the student experience has been defined narrowly by reference almost exclusively to teaching and learning.

While we have developed an increased understanding of teaching and learning and of its constituent parts (curriculum, delivery, assessment, etc) our understanding remains incomplete, to the detriment of the wider development of students. At the risk of overstating the position the orthodoxy could be summarized as being:

- Producer-led, that is, it proceeds on the basis that the (academic) staff know best. Prospective student needs are neither systematically researched nor acted upon. Thus students are not fully empowered and the retrospective evaluation of the student experience is imperfect and largely restricted to initial job outcomes.
- Discipline/subject/profession-based with a strong reliance, for the purposes of legitimation, upon external peer and other networks, including the 'invisible college'. Interestingly the apex of the British higher education quality assurance system, the external examiner system, is not universal.

- Based upon certain well understood, if ossified, notions of achievement and progression with attendant rites of passage, master-apprentice relationships and relatively narrow assessment regimes leading to hierarchically-certificated levels of achievement.
- Resolutely instructional if less didactic than previously.
- Campus-dominated, ie focused in and upon the physical resource base.

The dominance of this instructional curriculum raises the extent to which higher education is genuinely enabling, that is the extent to which higher education really is educational. A new higher educational agenda beckons.

Allen (1988, pp. 98–102) surveyed the mission statements of British chartered universities and indicates a general subscription to the following key objectives:

For individual students: cognitive learning, emotional and moral development; practical competence.
For the needs of society: the discovery, dissemination, preservation and application of knowledge; the provision of a focal point for the arts; the discovery and development of skills and talent.

The instructional curriculum and its pedagogy have incompletely addressed this agenda and the wider development of students is essentially implicit, not specified or planned for, not assessed or certificated and therefore not credited. Yet for the bulk of graduates who choose not to proceed with further study in the discipline, the recall of substantive disciplinary knowledge decays rapidly after graduation and it is the wider transferable skills which are the foundation of their subsequent careers and lifelong learning.

A proposed approach: the experiential programme

What follows is a proposal to augment but not replace the instructional curriculum with what I have termed an 'experiential programme' in order to address the imbalances identified above. This proposal is based on the development of the following four broad objectives designed to enhance the wider development of students:

- disciplinary knowledge;
- competencies;
- awareness; and
- dispositions.

Disciplinary knowledge

Much has been written about this matter since it is the anchoring and universal value of the higher education mission. However, some observations may be relevant.

- In the same way as there is a rite of passage for students, there is also a rite of passage for disciplines. What may appear to be a stable landscape is actually subject to periodic upheaval, eg the post-war emergence of engineering as a proper subject of study in Britain's older universities.

- The explosion of published output in all subjects and particularly in the sciences has meant that it has for some time not been possible, even for career academics, to keep track of all developments even within their discipline. Moreover, the notion that the undergraduate curriculum, even if wholly devoted to the acquisition of disciplinary knowledge, can 'cover' the subject is now clearly unsustainable, the introduction of M.Maths, M.Eng, M.Physics programmes notwithstanding.
- Graduate employers do not appear to regard 'specialist subject knowledge' as being at all important. Thus this category was ranked least important of 15 broad categories in a recent study (Harvey *et al.*, 1992) and further, 'employers, it appears, are not impressed with the specialist factual knowledge of graduates ... nor do they rate specialist factual knowledge as important ...' (Harvey, 1993, p.7).
- The acceptance of a modular course philosophy, which enables the combination of unlike subject fields, is testimony to the ability to break disciplinary hegemony.
- The increasing realization that the application of knowledge to real policy concerns requires an interdisciplinary address to fuzzy and ill-structured problems.

My central proposition then is not that there is no role for disciplinary knowledge in Mark II modular courses but that we have become overly reliant upon it as both the necessary and sufficient condition of graduation.

Competences

By this is meant the demonstration and validation that students 'can do' specified things. Such has been the interest in this area that it has even begun to impinge upon higher education. The 'things' that students might be expected to be able 'to do' have been variously described as: competences, competencies, skills, personal skills, personal transferable skills, enterprise skills, non-academic skills, employment skills, life-learning skills etc, etc. The Council for Industry and Higher Education has noted that 'employers will increasingly expect Higher Education to give a grounding in personal skills: communication; problem-solving; team-work; leadership' (CIHE, 1987).

In discussion of these matters within British higher education three types of response are frequently encountered:

- Outright rejection of the notion that they have any place.
- Acceptance that they do have a place followed rapidly by the declaration that 'We're doing it already'.
- Acceptance that they do have a place, that something is already being done about these matters but that, thus far, this is insufficient.

I subscribe to the third proposition which in many institutions, particularly those seriously applying Enterprise project funding, is now at the core of academic debate.

Awareness

My central proposition is that British higher education has largely failed to deliver on one of the key expectations of it. This is what Robbins described as 'that background of culture and social habit upon which a healthy society depends' (Robbins, 1963). The myopia of the disciplines, the instrumentality of students and the neglect by government have combined to crowd out essential awarenesses. What graduating student today (where these have not been part of their institutional curriculum) can demonstrate a rounded (if non-specialist) appreciation of: our physical environment; technology; aesthetics; economics and politics; history etc, etc? The list is seemingly endless. Yet it is these very awarenesses that:

- predicate and legitimate disciplinary knowledge;
- contextualize the policy agenda;
- give us our sense of time and place.

It is no longer fashionable, at least in the UK, to talk of citizenship. For myself the only response to the alienation and anomie now experienced by so many is to recognize our mutual interdependence and to find a *modus vivendi* which both recognizes and values diversity and binds us together in a common purpose. That higher education has, thus far, neglected this challenge is its greatest calumny.

Dispositions

Higher education has traditionally been rather coy about its expectations of students in terms of their attitudes and dispositions. In a liberal and plural society such clarification has been thought to be inappropriate either because these are essentially personal matters or, if not, because they are addressable only by an unwelcome degree of social engineering.

Of my four objectives this is, unarguably, the most contentious. I am, however, again reminded of the Robbins Report which argued that 'what is taught should be taught in such a way as to promote the general power of the mind' so as to train future leaders, particularly in the fields of politics and administration. My response to the points above is that we need to recognize that in the competences debate now under way, reference is frequently made to 'leadership', 'team-working', 'social skills' and the like, and further that all forms of education involve a degree of social engineering.

My argument is *not* that we will not continue to need to ensure the production of future scholars and that therefore those dispositions are irrelevant, rather that for most graduate employees in the 21st century they will not be (and probably never have been) sufficient. The relevant desirable dispositions might, *inter alia*, include the following:

- A propensity towards activity and proactivity.
- An awareness of and sensitivity towards others.
- The qualities frequently cited by major employers, namely: 'What all employers want are sparky people who make things happen. Most are

looking for successful disobedience, people who will step out of the safe square' (AGCAS, 1993); or what Sternberg terms 'practical intelligence' and 'tacit knowledge', ie, 'the ability to learn how to succeed at work' (*The Guardian*, 28 January 1993). In addition to the competences described above, Harvey has found that graduate employers attach greatest weight to '... commitment, energy, self-motivation, self-management, reliability, co-operation, flexibility and adaptability' (Harvey, 1993, p. 5).

Conclusion

My overall contention is in three parts. First, that each of these four objectives is capable of being operationalized in that they can be:

- specified, perhaps in terms of learning outcomes;
- planned for, in terms of structured institutional curricula and experiential programmes;
- hierarchically assessed, in terms of the achievement of negotiated learner agreements;
- validated for quality assurance purposes, certificated by records of achievement or profiles and credit-rated for transfer purposes.

Second, that it is the achievement of *all* of these objectives which should be regarded as being both necessary and sufficient conditions for the award of the first degree. Third, that it is proven flexibility and durability of Mark I modular courses that provides reassurance that the transition to Mark II modularity, characterized as above, is capable of delivering on this new agenda.

Whether the will to change in this or indeed any particular direction exists in higher education is in doubt. In my view very few universities are sufficiently insulated from the chill winds of the outside world to be able to stand aside.

To light the path, I offer in Figure 17.1 a heuristic which is adapted from a Canadian study of problem schools (Fullan and Hargreaves, 1990). As will be evident this is designed to focus the key elements of university mission so as to improve overall effectiveness. In essence the model offers a cyclical planning process proceeding from assessment through planning, implementation and finally to evaluation.

I invite the reader to assess the extent to which their own institution has made progress on any, or all, of these issues.

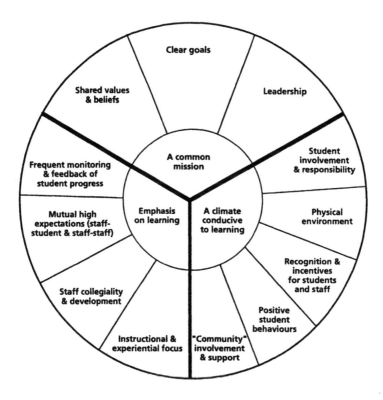

Figure 17.1 *Characteristics of effective universities* (after Fullan and Hargreaves, 1990)

References

Report of the Paul Hamlyn Foundation (1993) National Commission on Education, *Learning to Succeed: A radical look at education today and a strategy for the future*, London: Heinemann.

Allen, M (1988) *The Goals of Universities*, Buckingham: SRHE and Open University Press.

Harvey, L (1993) *Employer Satisfaction: Interim report*, Birmingham: Quality in Higher Education Project.

Harvey, L, Burrows A, and Green D, (1992) *Someone Who Can Make a Difference: Report of the QHE employers' survey of higher education graduates*, Birmingham.

Council for Industry and Higher Education (1987) *Towards Partnership: Higher education-government-industry*, London: CIHE.

Robbins Report (1963) *The Report of the Committee on Higher Education*, London: HMSO. CM 2154.

Association of Graduate Careers Advisory Services (1993) *What Do Graduates Do?*, West Sussex: Biblios.

Fullan, M and Hargreaves, A (1990) *What's Worth Fighting for in Your School? Working together for improvement*, Buckingham: Open University Press.

Chapter 18

Developing Local, National and International Credit Frameworks

Clive Robertson

Without visionary leadership, modular courses can become parochial and inward-looking, over-centralized and bureaucratic, bigger but not better, and centred on the course rather than the student. There is a danger that simply delivering a unitized programme becomes an end in itself. The opportunities offered by modular courses as Credit Accumulation and Transfer Schemes (CATS) to widen participation in higher education, encourage lifelong learning and develop European and international curriculum dimensions must be firmly grasped and actively promoted – to students and staff and to the community at large.

At a local level module courses such as CATS can be used to promote networking between colleges of further education through franchising, foundation and access courses, and through validation of modules. The definition of learning outcomes in terms of their credit value can facilitate partnerships between universities and local businesses through the recognition of work-based learning and the credit rating of in-company training. A modular course which describes the outcomes it expects students to achieve can capitalize on opportunities for articulation with the system of awards developed by the National Council for Vocational Qualifications in the United Kingdom. Learning outcomes provide a template against which the achievements required for National Vocational Qualifications (NVQs) and General National Vocational Qualifications (GNVQs) may be compared and then recognized for credit towards a university award. Thus universities can build bridges between different routes to qualification and help individuals move from NVQ to GNVQ to undergraduate, post-experience or postgraduate programmes. Only the universities themselves can offer this kind of flexibility of entrance to their programmes. An added benefit of this approach will be that we can identify those achievements which are particular to University programmes – the knowledge, skills and competences which characterize university graduates and which are not achieved through NVQs or GNVQs.

Modular courses such as CATS should be used to facilitate mobility of students within the UK, whether they are moving jobs as part-time students or simply taking advantage of mobility and opportunities to engage in particular areas of study offered by the flexibility of entrance to and exit from programmes of study. Consortia of universities can promote this activity but there is little evidence of this happening. Partnership and cooperation between universities in promoting CATS is difficult to achieve in the highly competitive climate of the 1990s. Such consortia together with colleges of further education and industrial partners can exploit to the full the opportunities which modular courses and CATS offer the individual learner.

Through active promotion of CATS, universities can commit themselves to the ambitions of the European Union which are framed in Article 126 of the Maastricht Treaty: 'mobility of students and teachers ... mutual recognition of academic qualifications ... cooperation between educational establishments ... exchange of information and experience in education practice ... development of language skills ...'. They can actively participate in educational developments within the European Union and, perhaps more essentially, provide staff and students with opportunities for career and personal development in the Europe of the future. To this end universities will need actively to pursue the goals of mutual cooperation and recognition of programmes of study and awards which will facilitate free movement of students and working people.

A modular course which provides full and explicit information to students about the learning outcomes they can expect to achieve, the ways in which they will achieve them, and the ways in which they will be able to demonstrate their achievements in a modular course which can actively develop CATS and promote student mobility, needs to be developed in the UK, in Europe and the wider world. Learning outcomes can provide the template against which other programmes of study and other awards may be measured. They enable a student to be proactive in planning and developing a profile of achievements including those from study abroad.

The promotion of CATS through modularizing courses and explicit definition of learning outcomes will help us to develop a style of higher education within the political, cultural and educational pluralism of Europe – a style enriched by this pluralism and not constrained by it – and which emphasizes and actively responds to the needs and expectations of the individual learner rather than being hindered by regulation and bureaucracy. Fundamental to this style is the need to recognize that although things may not be the same they may have equivalence, and consequently to accept approximation. Issues of jurisdiction must not be allowed to cloud the potential gains of mutual recognition based upon openness and accessibility of information. The style will evolve only if we are prepared to be proactive and pragmatic, to experiment and try things out while at the same time maintaining standards of quality against which we judge our efforts.

Collaboration between institutions of higher education in Europe and internationally currently takes various forms: non-reciprocated study or work placements, exchange of study or work placements, staff exchanges and joint research projects. At one end of a spectrum it may involve closely integrated curriculum design across a number of national boundaries, joint programmes of study with joint examinations and marking, and dual qualifications awarded to graduates. Such close integration requires lengthy planning, close cooperation and often complex bureaucratic solutions to issues of jurisdiction. The conventional model of the course submission document in the UK may prove difficult to obtain from another institution in another country and there may be an understandable reluctance by academics in one country to be scrutinized by external examiners from another educational system. At the other end of this spectrum a CATS philosophy allows the receiving institution to make judgements about the certificated and uncertificated prior learning of an individual, the appropriateness of this learning to its own programmes of study, and this admission to the programme with credit. As in the USA, the students' transcript or profile is their record of achievement and the 'trade-in' value of credits so far accumulated depends on the institution being approached and the course for which the 'trade-in' is being made.

The allocation of credit is, of course, fundamental to CATS. The CATS launched by the Council for National Academic Awards in Britain in 1986 was time-based, defining the full-time undergraduate year as equivalent to 120 credits; thus a first degree was 360 credits. Credits were available at four levels corresponding to the three years of a conventional degree programme, Levels 1, 2 and 3 respectively, and a postgraduate level M. A masters degree was defined as 120 level-M credits. This scheme has been widely adopted in the UK, though in many universities judgements of credit rating are increasingly influenced by the learning outcomes achieved as well as the time taken to achieve them.

In 1987 a CAT scheme was launched in Europe under the ERASMUS Programme of the European Council. The European Community Course Credit Transfer System (ECTS) equated an academic year to 60 credits and on a six-year pilot programme has involved some 145 institutions. The scheme was not to replace the successful Inter-university cooperation Programmes (ICPs) but to complement them. The latter programmes were designed to increase the number of students spending a recognized period of study in another European state but, despite rapid growth, an ideal of 10 per cent of students enjoying some form of transnational study has not been realized. Periods of study of three to 12 months are arranged through ICPs and staff mobility is also encouraged. In 1993/4, 2,135 ICPs were supported, with the UK remaining the largest partner country with about one-fifth of approved ICPs. Some 112,000 students are expected to study abroad in this year and 8,000 lecturers will take part in exchanges.

A guiding principle of ECTS is mutual trust and confidence in academic judgements made by staff in other institutions. There is a commitment to maximum flexibility and the avoidance of rigid rules which would hinder student mobility. Thus it reflects the four freedoms of movement – goods, services, capital and persons – provided for in the Treaty of Rome and the European Council's desire for transferability of higher education awards from one member state to other in the European Union through mutual recognition rather than harmonization.

The ECTS scheme is said to have been inspired by the example of Wim Mulder, a Dutch student who, after a first year of university education in the Netherlands (60 credits), moved successively to Germany, England and France accumulating a Diploma in Germany (120 credits), a BA in the UK (180 credits) and a Maitrise in France (240 credits) on the way, by claiming credit for his previous studies at each new institution he entered. This was seen as an example of true student mobility and a model for the future. Such a graduate could be open-minded, committed to Europe and have excellent employment opportunities. It is disappointing that in 1994 the fictitious Wim Mulder is still used to illustrate the ambitions of ECTS and there are no real examples to be quoted.

As mentioned earlier, student mobility is well established in the USA. A four-year bachelors degree is subdivided into 128 credit hours, 16 credits per semester. Twelve hours of laboratory class, for example, gain four credits while 12 hours of lecture or seminars gain 12 credits. The credit value and content of courses is published and the achievements of students are recorded on a transcript, including the credit awarded. If a student moves to another institution the specific credit recognized will depend on the education reputation of the last institution – the 'pecking order' of institutions is well recognized – the comparability of courses and the educational goals of the student. Thus there may be complete recognition of previously gained credit, partner credit recognition, or no recognition at all! Such mobility is slow to develop in Europe.

The Trans European Exchange and Transfer Consortium (TEXT) was inspired by a Europe-wide CATS and the realization that if it was to be achieved it would largely be up to the universities to do it themselves. It was established in 1988 and became the 'outer circle' of ECTS with direct funding from ERASMUS. It is active in sponsorship of ICPs based on credit transfer and encourages staff as well as student mobility. It has published guidelines on good practice in CAT, and establishes subject networks which include academics from within the European Union as well as from Central and Eastern Europe.

An important development of ECTS and TEXT has been attention to the difficult and sensitive issue of transfer of grades between institutions. A grade transfer scale has been developed which recognizes the particular grading approaches of different states. Thus students may obtain recognition for their achievements which can be reflected in the quality of the award they gain. Such transfer requires careful monitoring to ensure that students who are assessed abroad are treated equitably but this is a significant development of European and international CATS. It is a far cry from the traditional student exchanges where some credit was given for studies abroad but grades obtained could not contribute to a final award – and the distinct lack of mutual trust and recognition amongst educators which that reflected.

European CATS remains to be fully exploited and to achieve high levels of participation. The benefits of ECTS to staff and institutions as a whole as well as to individual students need to be actively communicated to decision makers in universities and further funding will be necessary to help institutions to adopt ECTS principles and mechanisms.

In the long term the philosophy of CAT and adoption of credit values to describe the outcomes of learning will facilitate student mobility and articulation between a range of learning opportunities. Credit Accumulation and Transfer is the single most important benefit of modularizing programmes of study. It will be more effective in widening participation in higher education in the UK, in Europe and the wider world than bilateral or multilateral agreements which must each be individually negotiated. A common credit framework, based on mutual recognition of credit will be attractive to students and employers in Europe and beyond. This will, however, only grow from a climate of mutual trust, confidence and recognition based on openness, the exchange of ideas and access to information. There is a great need for collection and dissemination of data about courses and credit ratings and this should be a primary function of ECTS and TEXT and of university consortia in the UK. Such data and case histories can be used to promote CATS in the future, to encourage the development of a modular higher education without frontiers and the recognition of work-based learning and university study, part-time and full-time study, open and distance learning, learning in any part of the world … Just think of the capabilities which students will derive if the full potential of CATS can be harnessed!

Index